POSITIVE WOMEN

VOICES OF WOMEN LIVING WITH AIDS

— Jane Shepherd

DESIGN FOR THE MASHAMBANZOU HIV/AIDS CRISIS CENTRE IN HARARE, ZIMBABWE. MASHAMBANZOU IS A SHONA WORD MEANING "THE TIME OF DAY WHEN THE ELEPHANTS WASH THEMSELVES." LESS LITERALLY IT MEANS, DAWN OF A NEW DAY.

POSITIVE
WOMEN

VOICES OF WOMEN
LIVING WITH AIDS

EDITED BY ANDREA RUDD
AND DARIEN TAYLOR

SECOND
STORY
Press

CANADIAN CATALOGUING IN PUBLICATION DATA

Main entry under title:

Positive women

ISBN 0-929005-30-9

1. AIDS (Disease) - Patients - Biography.
2. Women - Diseases. 3. AIDS (Disease) - Social aspects.
I. Rudd, Andrea. II Taylor, Darien.

RC607.A26P67 1992   362.1'969792.0082 C92-093780-2

Printed and bound in Canada

Edited by Sarah Swartz
Cover by Beverly Deutsch
Introductory graphics for each chapter by Andrea Rudd

Second Story Press gratefully acknowledges
the assistance of the Ontario Arts Council
and the Canada Council

Published by
SECOND STORY PRESS
760 *Bathurst Street*
Toronto, Canada M5S 2R6

A NEED TO BE

I need you my sistahs
help me re affirm my self
in my loving myself
hold me when I can't stand
from the pain weighted on my back
when the soles of shoes have travelled
on me for so long
I need you my sistahs

Imani Harrington

ACKNOWLEDGEMENTS

We are grateful for the help from the following: Canada Council's Exploration Program, Adam, Peter, St. Stephens A.I.D.E.S. Project, Community AIDS Treatment Information Exchange, Vivi Tobler, Bella Pomer, Doug Wilson, Liz Herlich, City of Toronto AIDS Prevention Programme, World Health Organization's Global Programme on AIDS, PWA Coalition Newsline, all of the newsletters that ran our call for submissions, all of the women living with AIDS who inquired about and supported this project, and Liz, Lois and Margie of Second Story Press.

We would like to acknowledge the work of Heidi Barrett-Jones for the translation of *Nicole Follonier*, *M. and Marie Werner*; Sylvana Bazet for the translation of *Rosa Guerrero*; Per Brask for the translation of *Inger M*; Marta Kovacs for the translation of *Maria*; Helen Monteiro for the translation of *Grupo Pela Vidda*; and Vivi Tobler for the translation of *Dina*.

WORKS PREVIOUSLY PUBLISHED

Lori Lynn Ayers, *Body Positive*, February 1991, Vol. 4, No. 2 (New York).

Iris de la Cruz, *PWA Coalition Newsletter*, October and November 1990, Issues 59 and 60 (New York).

Carole LaFavor, *PWALive*, March/April 1990, Vol.3, No. 2 (Minneapolis).

Grupo Pela Vidda, *ABIA's Bulletin* March and May 1991, Nos. 13 and 14 (Rio de Janeiro, Brazil).

Fran Peavey, *A Shallow Pool of Time: An HIV+ Women Grapples with the AIDS Epidemic* (New Society Publishers: Philadelphia PA, Santa Cruz CA, and Gabriola Island, BC; 800-333-9093).

Cate, *TASO Newsletter*, August 1990, Vol. 1, No. 1 (Kampala, Uganda).

Isabel and Dambudzo. "AIDS, An Issue For Every Woman", a report of the proceedings of the Women and AIDS Support Network Conference, November 1989 (Harare, Zimbabwe).

CONTENTS

INTRODUCTION

Both editors of this anthology are women who are HIV positive. Like all the women whose work is presented in this volume, we have the human immunodeficiency virus (HIV) that
is believed by many people to be the cause of AIDS.

Andrea and I met in 1989 at a support group for women
living with HIV and AIDS in Toronto. I had been attending
this group, made up of about a dozen women, for over a year
when Andrea joined us briefly. At first, my experiences in this
support group were very positive. I had never met another
HIV positive woman up to that point, and the excitement of
recognizing our mutual concerns had interesting results.
Together this group of women had written an article on
women with HIV for a local newspaper, and I had subsequently written an article on our group for *Healthsharing* magazine,
a Canadian feminist health journal. But a year later, I was
becoming very impatient with this model of support. Our
weekly meetings had, from my point of view, become vehicles
for long, often very depressing, monologues on what was
wrong in our lives, rather than how we could work to change
them. The group felt very isolated from concerns in the larger
HIV community, and I was beginning to question the fact
that the group was led by women who were not HIV positive
themselves. In short, it was time for me to move on.

Andrea arrived at this support group not long after she
had found out she was HIV positive. She was full of the
dynamism that a positive HIV test can give. Already she had
visited the offices of *Positively Women*, a self-help organization
for HIV positive women in England, and had ideas about cor-
responding with the women there. She had brochures from
Positively Women about how to live well with HIV, and she had

photos of the HIV positive women who worked in the offices there. One of the photos that was especially meaningful was of the big healthy HIV negative baby girl that one of these women had decided to have after she discovered that she was HIV positive. These were precious and revolutionary documents that were the beginning of our vision of this anthology and all of the work we have done since then.

In 1989, I had known that I was HIV positive for about two years. I had been working as a teacher in Zimbabwe in the mid-1980s and there was not a lot of accurate information available about AIDS in that country, particularly in the rural areas where I was living. I knew about AIDS mostly as the media presented it: as a "gay disease." It was only towards the end of the four years that I lived in Zimbabwe, that the extent of the epidemic started to be acknowledged. After the death of a lover, I realized that there was a very strong possibility that I was HIV positive. Months of incredibly painful and lonely procrastination followed before I decided to test for HIV in Harare, the capital city of Zimbabwe. A week or so later, back at my rural boarding school, I received a letter which notified me that I had tested positive for HIV. With the little information that I had, I assumed this meant I had a few years left to live.

Back in Canada, more extensive blood work determined that although I was HIV positive, I was also in very good health. This news was hard to take in at first, since I'd steeled myself to hear the opposite. Unlike Andrea, who immediately acted on her diagnosis, I took a long time to absorb all the implications, to figure out what I was going to do with myself and the rest of my life. Luckily, I have always had lots of gay men as friends, and it was through them that I began to get in touch with the community of people living with HIV and AIDS. With this group of people, mostly gay men involved in groups like the AIDS Committee of Toronto or AIDS Action Now!, I felt comfortable admitting that I was HIV positive. The support that they in turn gave me, and the challenges with which they presented me, made it easier, and certainly very exciting, to become increasingly politicized and public about being an HIV positive woman.

So I began to speak publicly at, for example, panel discussions for the Women and AIDS Project at the AIDS Committee of Toronto, to address pro-choice rallies about reproductive coercion of HIV positive women, to attend international conferences. I became co-chair of AIDS Action Now!, Toronto's AIDS activist organization.

In contrast, Andrea has always been quite private about being HIV positive. She is intensely focused on her HIV status but she directs much of this energy inwards, exploring exercise, massage, natural therapies and spirituality. Her first and immediate reaction upon being told by her doctor that she was HIV positive was to go out and buy a good cooking pot. Soon after that, she began to think about how HIV could be related to the creative work that she has always done. She spent a lot of time persuading me to join with her in thinking about such a project.

It took some thought before we decided on the idea of assembling an international anthology of works by women living with HIV and AIDS. We knew that whatever we did, it was going to be related to living with this modern virus. After some discussion, we understood that we wanted to know more about women and their responses to the AIDS pandemic, more specifically, about the women who live with this virus in their bodies. It seemed to us that amidst an avalanche of statistics, a barrage of safe sex information, lists of risk factors, stories about women who had acted as caregivers and educators, our stories – the stories of women who were living with HIV and AIDS — were precisely the stories that weren't being told. We wanted to tell our stories in our own words.

When we began this anthology, it was difficult to get any information about women with HIV or AIDS. We didn't know how to contact one another. We didn't know about our varied and similar experiences in living with this condition. We didn't know about our symptoms, whether or not we could have healthy babies, or about treatments that could be particularly useful to us. I always considered that I worked hard to inform myself about HIV, yet I can recall how I spent months lying night after night in my big Victorian bathtub, looking for Kaposi's sarcoma lesions on my body. I had no information to tell me that these lesions, though common in HIV positive men, occur very rarely in HIV positive women. And I recall the articles and brochures that well-meaning friends sent me, which discussed how women could prevent themselves from becoming HIV infected, when all I wanted was information about how to save my life.

Today women have more information at their disposal, particularly in North America and some European countries. There are newsletters for HIV positive women, articles on women's symptoms and treatments in the treatment newsletters that come out of the medical and PLWA (People Living With AIDS) communities. There is an increasing militancy about our reproductive options and our inclusion in trials of AIDS drugs. There is more interest from the feminist community, which has been slow to take up the issues of women with HIV and AIDS. But we have had to struggle for all of this information. In many instances, we have had to create it ourselves because we live in a society which is in denial about the links between women and AIDS. Women with HIV and AIDS threaten society's ideas about sexuality, particularly the sanctity of heterosexuality with its close ties to reproduction. We raise age-old fears about illness and death.

When the work of creating an international mailing list and translating our information into five languages was done, the thousands of calls for submissions finally mailed out, then came the anxious but mercifully brief period of waiting for responses. It was an anxious time because Andrea and I had very little idea of whether HIV positive women would ever find out about our project through the service organizations to which we had mailed our information, let alone whether they would respond. If HIV positive women in a major North American city like Toronto were so poorly organized and serviced, how would we reach women in places where there was even less of an infrastructure through which we could make contact? We considered the many barriers to women's participation: literacy, the need for anonymity, fears of discrimination, and the question of whether women identify strongly as HIV positive when they are living amidst other oppressions such as poverty, war, apartheid, etc.

We tried to foster a broad range of submissions by encouraging women to submit visual as well as written material, realizing that not all women are comfortable or able to express themselves in writing. We encouraged women to submit their work in their first languages which could later be translated into English. In order to advertise our project widely, we asked AIDS newsletters to publish our call for submissions and we were impressed by the cooperation we received.

In fact, women began to respond to the idea of this anthology quite quickly. Some women sent us their work immediately, some asked for more information, and others contacted us simply because they had never spoken to another HIV positive woman before. Even those who had no interest in contributing to the anthology often wanted to hear our voices and talk to us about their lives. From some women, we received photos and other bold proclamations of their identity as HIV positive women, while other women preserved their anonymity throughout months of correspondence by using a pseudonym and a return address in care of a trusted friend.

Our work on the anthology focused an enormous interest and goodwill on the part of many women and marked the beginning of an international community of women living with HIV and AIDS. These were women who were living their lives fully, despite the fact that they often found themselves in situations which offered little support, and in a social climate which tells people with HIV to prepare for illness and death. We also experienced the profound isolation, the deep fear and loneliness of HIV positive women, and understood better how much we need opportunities to connect and communicate with one another. Women whom we had never met talked with us on the phone long-distance for hours and some even came to Toronto to visit us.

As submissions to the anthology arrived in their various forms from fourteen countries – tapes, interviews, newspaper articles, handwritten letters and computer printouts, photos and videos – Andrea and I were transcribing, editing, translating, selecting and arranging media promotion and trying unsuccessfully to fundraise. We gave a lot of effort and energy to this project in a year when we both already had our work cut out for us with other full-time and part-time jobs, activism work, treatment and health concerns, not to mention the stuff of our daily lives.

Positive Women changed and succeeded beyond our imaginings. We never anticipated that we would be able to bring together such a wide variety of women's experiences. Working for the past few years with the gay community on AIDS issues has shown us that, when it really matters, people living with this disease come together and respond in a way that cuts across differences of gender, race, class and sexual preference. We believe that this anthology is another instance of this type of response. The fact that Andrea and I are both HIV positive gives us credibility, and I believe that women saw this anthology as an opportunity to come together in all our variety, to speak in one place in our many voices.

The pieces in this anthology are overwhelmingly affirmative. In some, this upbeat tone may seem to cover fears that are too raw and threatening to be expressed. In other cases, death and loss and separation are faced squarely, yet something of worth always remains. These voices, sometimes plain and uneducated, affirm the unusual and exceptional in women's lives along with the value of daily life. The most important lesson that we've learned while working on this collection is about the bedrock courage of women's daily lives, the vital decisions that we make without support, without sufficient information, often alone.

Most of the submissions that we received are included in this book. Some have been published previously, often in small newsletters published by people living with HIV and AIDS. Other pieces were created specifically for our volume. In our call for submissions, we encouraged women to send different styles of writing and various types of visual imagery. We hope that this variety documents the spectrum of voices that women use when they talk about living with AIDS, from the defiantly public to the intensely private. Both Andrea and I feel that the strength of this anthology lies in the eclectic, sometimes incongruous, differences and surprising similarities amongst the women who speak here. I think that it would be much less likely that one would tap into such variety amongst men who are living with HIV and AIDS.

But for all our efforts, there are women's voices that are missing. The absent voices have something to do with the lack of control that an editor has over her call for submissions: who receives it and who doesn't, who responds and who doesn't. But there are also women everywhere who, for reasons of discrimination and oppression, are not able to know their HIV status, or knowing it, are not able to speak about it.

In selecting the order in which works would appear in *Positive Women*, Andrea and I tried to highlight the differences and similarities amongst women. We often found ourselves working on the order of the anthology late at night in our tiny office, with forty different pieces of work on the floor in front of us, moving them back and forth across the length of the room until our eyes were glazed and our minds boggled. In our volume, some pieces follow one another as variations on a theme. Sometimes we juxtaposed different experiences and techniques. We found it impossible to group works by theme, and disliked the idea of grouping women together in categories which would divide us in the way that statistics and reports often do.

Each woman is identified as she wished, either with her real name, her initials, or a pseudonym, and by the country in which she lives. Decisions which women made about the names they use in this anthology are consequential ones. Frequently women spoke to us about their fear of losing their jobs, their friends and loved ones, their homes and their children if it were discovered that they are HIV positive. In our introductions to each piece of work, we have tried to give the reader a context and an understanding of the issues with which each contributor is grappling as well as, in some cases, what we know about the contributor through personal contact. We are by no means experts on the international context of AIDS, so our introductions don't contain the facts and statistics that some readers might find interesting. Throughout, our intent has been to focus on personal experiences.

Without a doubt, there are going to be words, opinions and decisions presented in these pages with which not everyone will agree. Often this anthology enters territory that society would prefer not to acknowledge or discuss. The reproductive rights of HIV positive women, for example, is an issue about which many people are divided. HIV positive women are often advised not to become pregnant because, it is reasoned, they will not live to raise their child, or they might give birth to a child who will develop AIDS. But in this anthology, the need that many HIV positive women feel to have children is presented repeatedly and with an immediacy that is very provocative.

Homophobia is not absent from this text, nor is incest, addiction or sexual abuse. AIDS often acts as a catalyst for women to begin to painfully examine their personal lives. The women who write on these pages do not always have safe sex, nor do they always use needles safely. Some of them are, or were, sex trade workers. AIDS also reveals the arbitrariness of the categories that society uses to regulate and identify sexual preference. Lesbians write here of having sex with men, straight women talk of having sex with gay men, and bisexual women try to move beyond a silence that they feel has been imposed on them by these categories.

But perhaps the biggest myth that *Positive Women* will explode is the myth that women don't get AIDS. Women from all walks of life, from all around the world can and do get AIDS. There is no profile; there are no risk groups here. We are women living with HIV and AIDS. This anthology documents our lives.

LORI LYNN AYERS
USA

Before she found out she was HIV positive, Lori was pursuing what she refers to as "the Great American Dream": — money, career, possessions, etc. HIV has given her the opportunity to reflect on her life and change it. She gave up her job in the film industry and the lifestyle that went along with it, and moved to the country in New York State.

Lori's perspective on HIV is that of an activist. She has written a number of articles for the Body Positive, a well-known newsletter for people living with HIV and AIDS, and she is a member of ACT-UP (AIDS Coalition to Unleash Power) in New York. In addition, Lori played a major role in the first American National Women and HIV Conference in Washington, D.C.

Lori's article is from the point of view of a woman with a number of choices for treatment, information and support. Therefore her tone is upbeat and optimistic, in contrast to the experience of many other women who have contributed to Positive Women.

Lori writes of herself: "I am 33 years old, ivy-league educated, born in Kansas, infected via a one-night stand. I'm a fighter and I don't want people to just give up and lay down and die."

A Year In The Life

Happy anniversary. It's a year now. No one was more shocked than I when I received my diagnosis. Hell, I hardly knew what HIV was. I just thought that my life, which had been pretty great to that point, was nearly over. My boyfriend of five years turned up negative and promptly informed me that he couldn't cope and wouldn't be around. I was alone and the sky was falling in. I didn't realize then what is so wonderfully clear now: that this diagnosis would turn out to be an incredibly positive force for change in my life. I'm not saying I'd prefer to carry this virus around in my body. But it's there and I appreciate the life lessons and changes that have happened because of it and am deeply grateful. I've learned and grown more this year than I ever would have, left to the complacency of my old life.

The first thing was to learn all I could about this virus, and there are plenty of resources out there for that. What I learned is that no one has the answers; no one really knows about the phenomenon that is human life. Western medicine is good at some things, but limited. I never realized before how medicine in this country provides a very narrow pathway to healing under the guise of protecting us from quackery. It is a monster gone out of control and is too heavily and too shamefully chained to the profit motive. Chinese medicine and many holistic modalities offer a different perspective that makes more sense on many levels. But your own mind and spirit centre makes the greatest difference of all.

At first I told no one I had the dreaded AIDS virus and that made it much harder. Fear grows and breeds when it is not faced. I was lucky in that I told my employer who was understanding and encouraged me not to hide the fact that I am HIV positive. As I told more people I realized how important it was to have honesty in my life about all things. Losing my boyfriend was a real blow. But I knew deep inside that our relationship had always been a compromise for me and not the closeness and complete sharing that I had wanted. Even my filmmaking career, though glamorous on the surface, was not anything I could really be proud of. The world needs more grade B movies about as much as it needs more litter. And so I started reaching out for what I really wanted, which was peace and harmony within myself and a sense of time and life not wasted. I started trying to become what I should have been all along. Because I thought I had forever, I had never examined my goals and what I really wanted out of life.

I had so much to learn about the virus, my own body's functioning and the politics surrounding the AIDS crisis. And as I learned, my life changed. My diet changed from the average American quick-fix garbage to a healthy and nourishing fare. I gave up all cigarettes, drugs and alcohol, and started exercising daily. This was not easy or immediate, but required courage and perseverance. I was rewarded by increasing self-respect and serenity. Now that I'm taking proper care of myself, I feel better than I have since I was eight years old. I am aware of my body and I treat it with respect and love and it responds by giving me joy. I don't know what the future may bring. But no one does and all anyone has is the present moment.

One door closes and another one opens. Finally out of the old relationship and open to change, I really did meet the man of my dreams and we are engaged now. He is HIV negative as were several men I dated who knew my serostatus. After a while I stopped being surprised that I didn't turn all men off. People are pretty well-informed about HIV/AIDS these days.

Determined to follow these new opportunities which were opening up for me, I quit my filmmaking job. Making those movies became relatively unimportant to me and certainly not worth the stress. I want to spend my energy to do some good in this world, to live in harmony with the world, not just batter my way through. Most HIV positive women are not as fortunate as I am to have the luxury of voluntarily leaving my job and changing my life.

Recently I attended the first National Women and HIV Conference in Washington, D.C. I never considered myself an activist and certainly never wanted to spend my time fighting the system. But at that conference it was impossible not to feel compelled to fight against the injustices of the current system toward women who have this virus.

The first night in one of the caucus rooms, I worked with other women to write a solidarity statement which focused on basic actions which the government needed to take immediately to help HIV infected women who have been largely ignored. I ended up being the one to present the statement to the conference and I asked other HIV positive women to read it aloud with me. Afterwards hundreds of conference attenders signed their copies and brought them to the government leaders present. I had never addressed a crowd before in my life, but it's not so hard when you speak from your heart .

It was a momentous occasion and a turning point when I found out I was HIV positive. No one knows how long one has in this world and it is a gift to realize that each moment is precious. It's too bad so many of life's lessons have to be learned the hard way. For me, I know that when I die I will be satisfied with my life as I have lived it, in a way that I might not have if I hadn't had this virus in my life. I will never give up hope and joy. I'll "survive" this plague, I have already survived it in that I can grow, learn and experience being alive today.

So many people were so lovely and helpful in the beginning when I was so scared. There's a lot of support out there. I am closer than ever to my family and friends. I've never had so much love in my life. And that's the great thing about love: the more you give away, the more you have. So hang in, reach out. It'll be okay.

ROSEMARY MULENGA
ZAMBIA

Rosemary delivered the following speech at the opening of a 1990 international AIDS conference in Paris, France. In it, she gives an overview of the impact of AIDS on Zambian women.

There are a number of differences between the situation of women and AIDS in Africa, and their situation in industrialized countries. In most African countries, AIDS has widely affected the general population: men, women and children. It is not confined to certain communities or socio-economic groups, as it tends to be in North America and Europe. Other factors that are specific to women and AIDS in Africa are the pressure on women to marry and bear children, the practice of polygamy and the economic pressures which often force women to have sex for money. Jane Shepherd's poster "Girls have the right to say no to sex" on page 177 illustrates these pressures.

Rosemary was formerly a school teacher, but resigned her job after finding out she and other members of her family were HIV positive. Very active in her church, Rosemary introduced AIDS education to her congregation and later came out publicly as a woman living with HIV. She became an inspiration to other families living with the challenges of AIDS.

I come from a country called Zambia. Zambia is a beautiful country set in the warm heart of Africa. It is slightly larger than France in size, but our population is estimated at between 8 and 10 million, with approximately half the people living in towns and cities. Zambia is the most urbanized Black African country. This has many social consequences and is especially significant in the context of AIDS.

The first cases of AIDS were identified in Zambia in early 1983. In 1986, AIDS was declared a public health problem. Today AIDS cases fill about 25 to 50 percent of the beds in many urban hospitals and the problem is likely to get worse in the future. About 25 percent of women attending antenatal clinics in the urban areas of Zambia are HIV antibody positive. Lusaka, the capital city where I and my family live, has a population of over one million people. It is estimated that over 65,000 childbearing women could be infected in the next few years with disastrous consequences. The mortality rate of children under five is expected to increase by at least 25 percent, wiping out the hard-earned gains of our child survival programs.

Now I would like to say a little about AIDS and me, how AIDS got into me and how my life has since changed from that of victim to victor. I consider myself to be an average middle class Zambian woman. My husband Oliver is a journalist. I used to work as a teacher. We are no different from other Zambian families except that we are HIV positive. I was diagnosed positive in January 1987 after being ill for about four months with hepatitis B. My husband and my now five-year-old son were also found positive. We were shocked and anxiety filled our lives: fear of early death and especially who will look after our four children if we died. You know, those sort of questions became real to us. We have not been courageous enough to tell our children about it yet. We have

27

managed to tell our parents and brothers and sisters and a few friends, although they would not accept it as true. We have received a lot of support from the church and the support group to which I belong.

Since my condition, my life has become more real and fruitful. I and my husband have helped to form an HIV/AIDS support group in the city of Lusaka. About 20 people meet every Saturday to support one another. I am involved in giving educational talks to church women and school children on AIDS and I try to get them involved in the care of the sick and children in distress. I believe that God has given me a message for the church and other organizations, challenging them to confront AIDS positively. I also believe that God has sent me to help the suffering women in Zambia who are hurting because they have the disease or have lost a relative by it. I have a heart of compassion and empathy, because I identify with them. I always try to comfort them with the same comfort I myself have received from God and from friends. Most important, I take the pleasure of introducing them to Jesus Christ, who alone can offer absolute peace of heart, forgiveness of sin, restoration and, of course, healing and hope for living.

As I counsel more and more women about AIDS, I have become more interested in the issues of women and AIDS. I would like to highlight some of the issues that women in Zambia are facing today. Women are very vulnerable to HIV infection for several reasons. Traditionally the status of a woman has been lower than that of a man. The man was seen as the hunter and the woman as the conquest. In modern times things have not gotten any better. Women make up the greater percentage of those who cannot read or write in Zambia. As a result, there are relatively very few women in formal salaried employment.

Within a relationship, it is usually the man who chooses his partner and controls when to have sexual intercourse with her. A woman who is worried about HIV infection or sexually transmitted diseases cannot refuse to have sex with her husband or insist that he use condoms. Accommodation supplied by the government or even by a private company usually belongs to the man. So the need for a home and money to buy essentials for her children and herself often forces the wife to stick to a degrading marriage situation. This unfair situation exists not only in marriage. Young girls are pressured to have sex. There is the sugar daddy, who exploits the innocence and the economic vulnerability of young girls. There is also intense social pressure on single young women to be married. This pushes them into relationships with men whether or not the men are single or married, in order that the women can somehow be counted among those with the status of marriage.

Traditionally, an African woman has her ultimate fulfillment in childbearing. The goal of every woman is to leave behind one or more children for her family or tribe, irrespective of whether she is married or not. If a woman has no children or has only girls, then she will be under considerable pressure to continue childbearing, whether or not she is carrying HIV. Within a marriage, a woman doesn't have much say in issues such as child spacing or family planning, despite the fact that it is her body that is being used for childbearing and childrearing.

Zambia is going through a hard economic period. Women, both married and single, are suffering from the impact of high inflation and lack of formal salaried employment. Many of them are involved in petty trading to raise some money in order to survive. In this situation, the pressure to have sex for money is very high. Because the government does not want to acknowledge that prostitution exists, there is little help when single women demand treatment for sexually transmitted diseases or contraceptives at government clinics. As you can see, the woman in Zambia, the woman in Africa, the woman in the third world, the woman in the world at large is much more vulnerable than a man to HIV infection.

In addition, AIDS is yet another enormous burden to the Zambian woman. Family involvement in the care of the sick at home is common in our culture. At the centre of all care is a woman, either as wife, mother, aunt, sister, cousin or even a grandmother. It is the woman who feeds, who washes, clothes and cares for the sick and the dying.

My message to women everywhere is that we must not wait for others to fight our battles for us. I am HIV positive, but AIDS has not beaten me. I will fight this monster and its effects on me personally, on my family and on my community, as long as I am alive. Sisters, reach out to your sisters, and let us remember that when you teach a man, you teach an individual, but that when you teach a woman, you teach and reach a nation.

THE WOMEN OF GRUPO PELA VIDDA

BRAZIL

The following conversation was recorded specifically for Positive Women *by the women of* Grupo Pela Vidda (Group for Life) *in Rio de Janiero, Brazil. It is translated from the Portuguese. We decided to preserve as much as possible the informal style of the conversation.*

Grupo Pela Vidda *is a support group for people affected by AIDS and sponsored by ABIA, the Brazilian Interdisciplinary Association. Its members include women of various ages intimately affected by AIDS. This means that not all the women who speak here are HIV positive. They may be related to others who are.*

This piece is unique in the anthology because the women speak so openly about their continued sexuality as women with HIV. As in many African countries, in Brazil AIDS has severely affected the heterosexual community. Thus the women who speak here are grappling with AIDS in a heterosexual context in a society where sexuality is openly accepted.

Zia: Women have always been discriminated against. When a woman tells her partner that she has AIDS, he runs away. He goes to another experience. And she stays alone.

Patricia: Did you ever have a man after you found out you were infected?

Zia: Yes. I told him and he left. I couldn't go to bed with a man keeping this kind of secret. He said that he didn't use condoms, that I should look for another partner who could accept them. Because as much as he tried, he couldn't.

Marta: I had three different experiences. To the first man, I didn't say anything. I only insisted that we use condoms and he accepted this without a problem. But after a short while, he found out that my husband had died of AIDS. Even though he had used condoms, he came looking for me. I heard that he was armed; I heard many stories...

The second experience was completely different. He knew my husband. I haven't done anything with him, we have only gone out together. I told him that I am HIV positive. And even so, he wants to go out with me. But I can't. I will not stay with a person just to have his company and to have sex, if I don't love him.

The other man is a policeman. I only met him a few days ago. We went for a beer, and we talked. We talked about a friend whose husband is in jail. Then he said, "If I was the wife of a bum who went to jail, I would leave him, because there is a lot of AIDS in jail. AIDS disgusts me." Then I thought to myself, I cannot tell him that I am HIV positive. But later on, when we were more intimate, I said, "If you are so afraid of AIDS, why don't you use condoms?" He said, "I am not going to use those things, no way." I said, "So, you are not afraid. If you were afraid you would use condoms. Take me as an example. Do you know anything about me? Do I know anything about you? You don't know whom you are with." He answered, "No, I don't know." I said, "It's right to use condoms. If we are going to be together, I insist on using condoms. Furthermore, I think you move too fast. You don't even know who I am." He answered, "Okay, you are so wonderful that I will buy a box of condoms."

He was supposed to call me yesterday, but he didn't. Maybe he thought about it and got frightened. This is the way I try to proceed. I don't tell the truth because the truth makes the person run away. But I look for other ways of guaranteeing that the person will not be at risk: using condoms, having safe sex.

Patricia: So your position is to never say that you are infected?

Marta: Yes. This is very difficult. And you are going to lose many men, the ones you want. Both cases that did not work out well for me were people with whom I felt comfortable.

It is not that I want a commitment from anyone. It's not even sex. But I miss some affection. But no man will give affection to you with 36 years on your face without asking for sex.

Sonia: Usually an HIV positive person needs to work out his or her sexuality. Since I came to the *Grupo*, with the number of activities I took on, my sexual desire has diminished. This is sublimation. Freud explains it, right?

Zia: It also happened to me. I don't feel the need for sex anymore. Even before I found out that I was HIV positive, I already wanted to be alone. I had so many bad sexual experiences, that I thought it would be better to be alone. I don't know if this is the right way, but it is better to be involved in many activities and not to let sex bother me day and night.

Veronica: My boyfriend said that he was infected. Now, after some months, I found out that he is not infected.

Xica: That is what he said. Do you believe him?

Veronica: Yes, I do.

Xica: Do you believe he wanted to get infected?

Veronica: Yes. He had sexual intercourse with me, so he could get infected.

Xica: You met this person through an ad in the paper, didn't you?

Veronica: Yes. He said he was HIV positive in the ad.

Xica: So, he was looking for an HIV positive woman.

Veronica: Yes. Now, he says he doesn't want to have sex with me with condoms. He wants to have sex without condoms.

Xica: Are you still with him?

Veronica: I am, but I think that I will not be with him for much longer. I don't want to have guilty feelings, if he gets infected.

Xica: And you? How is your life after you found out that you were HIV positive?

Isaura: I felt that a tractor passed over me. I hate my husband, and I love him at the same time. I want to kill him and I want to be close to him. It is very confusing. It seems that I am going crazy.

Patricia: What is this hate?

Isaura: Hate because I have always been loyal to him. He always had his freedom and his own life. Now, this happens to me.

Patricia: So, you hate him because you believe he infected you?

Isaura: I am sure about that. I only had him. When he was sick, we loved each other very much. Then, when I found out what he had, I started to hate him.

Patricia: Is your husband alive?

Isaura: Yes, he is.

Marta: Ah, your feelings will change. My husband loved me very much. And I was very loyal to him. He used to do drugs before being with me. When he was with me, he said that he was not doing drugs any more. I thought I was very mature and experienced, and I believed him. I don't know if he was already infected or if he got infected after being with me. When he got sick, I started feeling a maternal love for him, even in face of the disease. I loved him and I wanted him. But eventually I couldn't take it any more. I was always crying, always afraid of his crises. I started to wish he would die soon. Then I felt I couldn't live without him. How could I have wished that he would die soon? I couldn't understand what I wanted.

The doctor said that I had to remain calm, but how could I? I had to take care of him as well as my six-year-old son, my daughter and myself. I wished that someone would take my daughter and my son away. I didn't know what I wanted.

My husband died and now I miss him very much. When he was sick, he told me that he already knew he was positive for more than two years, that he had denied to himself that he was putting me at risk. He was afraid of losing me because he loved me very much. And I forgave everything. I loved him too much.

Beatriz: Of all the women I have told about my being HIV positive, no one ran away. They all have showed solidarity with me.

Maria: I feel happy! I have a lot of friends. We go out, we have fun, we go to bars, to lambadas. I just don't stay out all night any more. At two in the morning, I am at home, and they are still out there. I don't miss not having a boyfriend. There are even a lot of candidates, but I am not interested. Before I let the disease run my life. When I went out, I was afraid of the rain. But now I live normally. Just because it rains, am I going to catch a cold? No, I don't live like this anymore. Now I have lots of fun.

Beatriz: I also improved a lot after finding out I was HIV positive. I used to stay home watching TV. I was too lazy to go out, or even to dress myself. Now, when I am at home doing nothing, I think: "I don't know how much time I have left. I am going out. I am going to live." I go out more often. I take better care of myself. I know that what counts is today. I have begun to like myself more and to do things that I like. I am closer with my daughter and with my mother. I want to say something to you, Isaura, whose husband is alive. Try to give him all the love you can, all the attention. It doesn't help to want to die first. I also wanted it, but he died first because he was already sick. Give him all the love you can, because when he passes away, you will feel that you could have done more. I think all the time that I could have done more for him.

Margarida: I felt disgusted when I found out I was HIV positive. I felt like throwing myself under a car. I got really depressed. Because I am sure that my fiancé, who died, knew he had AIDS. He didn't tell me anything. When he died, the doctor called me because I had a high chance of catching AIDS or tuberculosis. I did the tuberculosis test and the result was positive. Then came the AIDS test. When the doctor told me the results of the test, I was calm. Then, afterwards, it struck me. I had never been sick before. I have been to the hospital only to deliver my children. And now, I live from hospital visit to hospital visit! I feel better, but at the beginning, I didn't even want to take a shower.

Monica: When my husband died, everybody checked me out and asked, "Aren't you sick?" And I answered, "No, thank God, I don't have anything." Three months, almost four, have passed. Whereas I had been too thin, now I have even gained weight. And the people – the neighbours – look at me invitingly. The bakery owner, the store owner, they think I don't have anything anymore. It is like that. They think I didn't die within one month, so I don't have AIDS.

Dora: I am not open about being HIV positive because of my daughter. I am afraid that she will not get a boyfriend because they will be afraid of her, since her mother has HIV.

Rebeca: At school, if the teacher talks about AIDS, I say that I have many books about it at home. The other kids ask me, "Why do you have all these books?" I answer that on my street a man died of it and that now everybody tries to learn more about it. Then they ask to borrow my books. But usually they are not serious. They say, "You are too thin. Get out of here. You have AIDS." They don't know that also a fat person can have AIDS. The young people say, "I think I don't have it, because only gays and prostitutes get it. I will not catch it. We know each other. We know where we live. We know each other's families." I can't talk too much about it, because I am afraid they will ask me questions and find out about my mother.

Angelica: In my case, I have three teenage sons. Their father is infected and most people know it. I appear in the newspapers and on TV. My sons ask me not to appear in public. They fear people will think that because their father is infected, they are also infected. I think that because they are men it is more difficult for them to deal with the disease, because AIDS is connected to homosexuality and bisexuality. They close themselves to the subject. I have to respect their privacy and not invade their space. I believe they deny it and this bothers me, a mother of teenaged sons, because teenagers are exposed to a lot of things, mainly drugs and their first sexual experience. We know that they can get infected in their first sexual contact and it becomes very difficult if they won't talk about it. AIDS is part of our daily lives. I imagine how hard it is for people and families who do not have AIDS to talk with their children about it.

Marta: If the things we are talking about here were discussed everyday on TV, it would help a lot.

Miriam: There is a important point to be mentioned here. That is the need for HIV positive people to announce to the world: I am HIV positive and I am healthy. People must realize that being healthy doesn't mean that a person doesn't have the virus. Too often the inaccurate belief is that if you have the virus, you will immediately start deteriorating, losing weight, getting sick.

Marta: For me, AIDS has two kinds of prevention: not getting infected and not getting sick.

Julia: Something happened to me at the hospital. I went there to have an x-ray and I met a seropositive man who was also having an x-ray taken. We were waiting in the line and he said that he couldn't come to the *Grupo Pela Vidda*'s party but he asked for the telephone number and address. When I was writing it, the technician called him to take the x-ray.
    When I was called to take my x-ray, I asked the guy to wait for me. The technician looked at my paper and saw the word "SIDA" (Portuguese for AIDS). I think he didn't even know what AIDS or SIDA meant. When he touched my head to position it for the x-ray, he said, "You know, that guy who just left, he has AIDS." I said, "Me too." The technician got embarrassed, and said, "Sorry." I think he was afraid that I would tell the guy what he said. I asked him, "If you are so afraid of getting AIDS, do you use condoms?" He answered, "No. Me? Why should I use condoms, if one can get it from kissing, from tears, from sweat." Then, I said, "So, you better

be careful because you are touching my forehead. It is hot and I am sweating." He was very embarrassed. I felt I had to say something else. But I realized that he was so misinformed that the few minutes we had together would not be enough to make him understand. I would like to bring some educational material for him.

Patricia: He broke confidentiality. He could be prosecuted because of that incident.

Angelica: There is too much misinformation. My husband had diarrhea and strong fevers. So his boss told him, "You should take an AIDS test. My son died of AIDS and he used to have diarrhea and strong fevers. My husband said, "I am not gay." The boss said, "It's not only gay men who get this disease. You don't know what your wife is doing." Then he decided to take the test. I even asked him, "Why are you taking this test? You aren't gay. Don't you trust me?" Although he had had many women before me, he used to say that the women he had been with are all alive and everything is okay with them. Then he took the test and the result was positive. He didn't believe it. I continued to have sex with him without condoms. The family also wouldn't believe it. They said the result was a mistake.

Tonia: You saw how I was when I came here the first time — very depressed and often crying. I didn't have anyone to talk to because I thought that people would withdraw from me if I told them the truth. Even my mother avoids the topic. She says, "You are happy, satisfied, so shut up." We need to stop and talk to people who are going through the same problems, because other people don't understand them.

Before I found out I was HIV positive, my life was very

crazy, completely disorganized, with no time to eat or sleep. Now I am taking better care of myself, watching my health, being careful when sharing needles. I was even at a clinic trying to stop using drugs. It was there that I learned I was HIV positive. I asked for the test because I suspected that someone was using my syringe. In my house, people came in and out all the time. I use to leave my syringe on top of the sink. I didn't worry about it.

I still go out, go to parties. I go out with my friends, but I don't tell them everything.

Patricia: How do you and your friends who used drugs see the problem of AIDS?

Tonia: The important thing is always the drugs. Nobody wants to talk about AIDS. As long as they have the drugs, they don't care if there is only one syringe. Some people I know do not share their needles. There are other people who have money to buy more than one syringe, but they buy only one in order to infect others: "Ah! If I am going to die, I want everybody else to die also." I think this is a very wrong attitude. People must take initiative and stop contaminating other people. This is the minimum a person can do as a human being, in terms of human solidarity.

Patricia: And the circle of friends you used to have?

Tonia: That circle of friends has dissolved. They all went their separate ways. One is in jail in Petropolis and he injects even in prison because his nephew brings stuff to him. He is the kind of person who would take drugs and give the syringe to the first person he saw.

Patricia: What about the sexual behavior of people who are using drugs?

Tonia: Drugs and sex are not a good combination. Cocaine cuts the sex drive. For women, it completely cuts the desire. But after the effect of the drug is over, the first thing I thought about was a cigarette, drinking or having a very good man that I liked by my side.

I am involved with the fight to inform people about AIDS. I told my sixteen-year-old sister, "I have some condoms for you." She looked at me surprised. I told her that it doesn't matter if she is a virgin or not. That is her personal thing. I said, "I just want you to get informed and to inform your friends. You should consider me, your sister, your source of information.

Yara: The woman who employs me as her housekeeper doesn't discriminate against me. On the contrary, she is very supportive. She worries a lot about my health. She is like a mother to me. I think, "I will die before you, I will die and you will look after my kids." I love her. I eat at the same table as her, use the same plates. There is no discrimination.

Patricia: Everyone thinks that the sick person is the one who contaminates others.

Yara: On a TV program, it showed a HIV positive baby and a doctor who was wearing a mask and gloves. The program didn't explain that he was wearing a mask and gloves to protect the baby. No, people got the wrong message that the baby might contaminate the doctor. The problem is the lack of knowledge. Only HIV positive people will be able to reverse this situation.

Patricia: Instead of inhibiting the spread of the HIV, what they did was to awaken the disease called discrimination.

Yara: My husband died of both depression and discrimination. He didn't die of AIDS. He was HIV positive, had tuberculosis and recovered from it. He came back home and started thinking only about AIDS. He was a very "macho" man. People think that because he was in prison, when he was there he was a woman. But it is not true. He did drugs. People wondered, "What happened? Did his wife sleep around?" He had all this on his mind, as well as the lack of money, his own suffering, then my positive test. Imagine him finding himself condemned to die, and seeing the person he loves, who took care of him, also condemned. He got depressed, he wouldn't take medicines, he wouldn't eat. He entered a convulsive crisis, went to the hospital and died ten days later. On his medical report, it says that he died of AIDS because he had a positive HIV test. But he only had biliary tuberculosis that had been treated two months before. He had gained weight and he didn't have any other infection. He died of depression and discrimination.

Patricia: What made you take the test?

Yara: I had a flash. I went to buy a sink for my house near *Frei Caneca* Street. My house was being renovated. Coincidentally I was in front of the gay men's health centre. Then I thought since I was here, I would go in for a test.

Patricia: So, you trusted your husband?

Yara: Yes, I trusted him. But I was afraid. I think that if I had not been there that day I wouldn't have taken the test. Afterwards I didn't take a shower for one week. I wouldn't even go out on the porch. I stayed alone in my house which was a mess.

Marta: My son is 12 years old. Today we were having lunch at my mother's house and she started arguing and accusing me, "It is not my fault you have this problem. You got this problem by yourself." I said, " What is this, mom? We can't be sure about how I got infected. I may have gotten infected during the surgery I had. If a car hits an HIV positive person and some blood spills on you, you could become infected, God forbid it. But you wouldn't be able to avoid it. I am not guilty of being sick! When a person gets hepatitis, as is the case of Uncle Batista, he quarantined himself in the maid's room because he loves us and doesn't want to contaminate us. Do you think I want to contaminate you? I don't want to contaminate anyone."

Later my son asked me, " Mom, is it true that you have AIDS?" Then, my mother said, "No, she doesn't. It is all because of that surgery she had. It was a bad surgery." So, behind my mother I made signs to my son to agree with her and I also agreed with her. Later on, I told him that I am HIV positive, because I believe he has the right to know the truth. He is already a young man; he hugs the girls in the elevator. So he needs to know about these things. I'd rather he learns about them from me.

Yara: I told my son Cristiano about everything. I myself keep the glasses separate, everything. Sometimes when I am eating, Cristiano says, "Mom, give me a bite." I used to say, "No." He would say, "Why?" Then he would come and take some. You understand? He doesn't worry. I am the one who has it.

WENDI ALEXIS MODESTE
USA

Wendi was the first woman to contribute to this anthology. She is an African-American woman who lives openly and proudly with AIDS. Born into a middle-class family in Brooklyn, New York, she began using drugs at a very early age and became addicted to heroin and cocaine. In 1989, she got off the streets and kicked her addictions after she joined the Episcopalian Church. A year later she was diagnosed HIV positive. This diagnosis and her new found faith gave her a mission and a reason to go on living: to educate the public by putting a face to AIDS.

Wendi has become extremely active in AIDS education in New York State and was recently honored with the Women of Courage Award *from the City of Syracuse for her work. She writes prolifically for several AIDS newsletters, speaks publically about AIDS and does radio and TV interviews. Recently we were happy to meet Wendi after we helped to arrange for her to come to Toronto to speak to the Black community about women and AIDS.*

The following three pieces are by Wendi.

WENDI ALEXIS MODESTE

My name is Wendi Alexis Modeste. I'm a 37-year-old Black female. I now reside in Syracuse, New York, but I was born and raised in Brooklyn, New York. For many years, I literally lived on the streets of Harlem and the South Bronx.

At the age of 15, I began using illegal drugs intravenously. I came from a very intact upper middle class Black family. Both my parents were college educated. My father has a Masters of Social Work and is executive director of the Urban League of Onondaga County. My mother, now deceased, was an elementary school teacher. I have a sister Rhea Aloise who sets up wellness workshops for the elderly. I have two brothers. Keith André is a landscape artist. My other brother Leon Adrian is the athletic director for Phillips Academy, a very prestigious prep school (Both President Bush and Humphrey Bogart attended school there.)

No one in my family even smoked a cigarette. I did enough for everyone. My problem, I believe, was poor self-esteem. So I chose a lifestyle and people who were so far removed from the way I was raised that no one could compare me to the Modeste family.

I prostituted, stole anything not tied down, and continued the downhill cycle of addiction for more than 20 years. I started with IV heroin, then cocaine and heroin mixed (speed-balling), then plain cocaine and methadone, then crack. Kicking methadone, which was supplied by the state to help you get off heroin, was probably the hardest. My bones hurt for a long time. Crack was easiest to kick because I never really liked it. Eventually I landed in jail. The truth of the matter is it really didn't make any difference. I was glad to be taken in somewhere.

In July of 1989, I came to Syracuse to visit my daddy and stepmom. They had invited me to spend a couple weeks with them to get a rest, clean up, etc. My brother Keith was bringing his son up for a visit so I rode in the car along with them. Two months prior to that I'd tried to commit suicide. I was hospitalized in the psychiatric ward. It was one of many such hospitalizations. Anyway, while visiting Syracuse I went to church with my stepmom. It was July 21, 1989. For the first time in my adult life, I had a sense of well being. I felt the spirit of the Lord.

Soon after, I returned for a week to the horror of my life in New York City. For the first time, I realized I was better than the hell I'd created in my life. I had only one girlfriend who really cared about me and never wanted anything from me. She helped me get my thoughts together. After ten days in New York, I returned to Syracuse. I immediately got my own apartment, furnished of course. I began psychiatric outpatient counselling in October 1989 and soon after found out I had cervical cancer.

On February 12, 1990, I had a hysterectomy for treatment of cervical cancer. As I'd told my surgeon about my past life style, he ordered an HIV test on me. When I returned to my room but was still a bit groggy from anaesthesia, my surgeon came to see me. I asked him my prognosis. He said, "Well, as far as the cancer, excellent." He felt he got it all. But I had tested positive for HIV. The next day he came to see me again and since I hadn't really been coherent the day before, I questioned him again. He confirmed I'd tested positive for the AIDS virus. Then he told me after six weeks of abstinence from sex, if I decided to have intercourse, my partner should always wear a condom. He then told me he was going on vacation and an associate of his would check on me for the remainder of my stay. I thought his advice about sex was very inappropriate, as very few women who've just had all their reproductive organs ripped out through their stomach are thinking about sexual intercourse.

I did a whole lot of praying. I knew the Lord hadn't brought me through 20 years of self-loathing and destruction to die once I'd felt His word. I knew He had something He wanted me to do, so I listened. Once I was on my feet, I began reading everything I could get pertaining to HIV infection and AIDS. I contacted the Central New York AIDS Task Force. I joined a support group there. Then I heard the Red Cross was offering a course for people to become HIV/AIDS educators. I got into the course and passed with flying colours. I then took training to be on the Speakers Bureau at the AIDS Task Force in Syracuse. I also volunteered my time for office work and visiting other clients.

Soon it became clear to me what the Lord wanted. It was time to put a face to this disease. I spoke at the Women and AIDS Advisory Committee meeting on June 1, 1990 and they asked me to join. I explained to them I wanted to go public and let people see the human side of this illness. I speak all over Onondaga County to whomever invites me and, in addition to basic AIDS 101, I give a personal presentation. I find this to be very effective, as people respond well to the personal approach. Doing it this way, I'm also able to explain the hell drug abuse is. I show my scars and let them know that for the average person, it's not as easy as entering the Betty Ford Clinic periodically.

I realized during my education about HIV/AIDS that I'd been infected at least as early as 1987. I had a ten-and-a-half hour operation back then and was put in isolation. No one told me why. I asked, "Do I have AIDS?" and was told no by the doctors and nurses at Harlem Hospital. I then came down with herpes zoster and what I now know was a bout of Pneumocystis Carinii pneumonia, an AIDS defining illness. And still no one told me. In my ignorance, I lost two years of my life. I don't want that to happen to anyone else. That's why I advocate education as loudly and as often as I can.

Last week I went to a public hearing of the county legislature here. When it was my turn to have the floor, I told them that while my being a person living with AIDS might not concern them, the fact was that when I was ignorant of being HIV positive, I continued risky behavior which could have infected others. Education is our only defense right now. To cut funds for HIV/AIDS education is ludicrous. I joined the committee to plan AIDS Awareness Month here. I made up the slogan for our posters and stickers: "HIV/AIDS — Even if you're not infected, you will be affected." I've done two TV interviews and am doing another one this week. I'm also doing a radio interview. The Episcopal Bishop has appointed me to the National Episcopalian AIDS coalition. I gave a presentation at my own church and am doing others around the diocese.

People ask me how can I believe in the Lord, when after I accepted Him I was diagnosed as having cancer and AIDS. I tell them what scares me is to think about what it would have been like to receive this diagnosis without knowing Christ.

Because I believe in the Lord, I'm not afraid to die and when my work here for Him is done He'll be taking me home. Beside my mom's in heaven waiting for me and I really miss her.

SPEAKING TO THE LORD

Lord, I'm feeling mighty lonely
    but I know you're by my side;
Lord, I'm feeling down and desperate
    this from you I cannot hide.

Lord, my body's trying to fail me
    my bones ache and I feel weak;
So I come to you my father
    for the comfort that I seek.

I close my eyes to concentrate
    so I can feel your voice;
Then reaffirm my love for you
    and the fact you are my choice.

I feel your warmth surround me
    like a large protective hand;
I know one day I'll be with you
    in a far, far better land.

But here on Earth to do Your work
    I'll go to any length;
Because in my Mommie's favourite words,
"Lord, I know You'll Give Me Strength."

Dearest Mommie,

There is never a day I don't think about you or miss you. These past few days though, the pain of death is so strong it's almost tangible. We always need our mothers, no matter how old we get. I'm almost 40 and it's been nine-and-a-half years since you died. I'm supposed to be over it. Perhaps part of it is that it's the Christmas season. I've been through this season before and it hasn't been so melancholy. Maybe it's because I'm really sober and am now truly feeling the void left by your death. Mommie, I'm so sorry for the 20 years of hell I put us all through, but especially you. If I hurt anyone more than myself, I know it was you. How I wish you were here so I could lay my head on your bosom and feel your arms around me. I always felt so safe and secure like that.

Mommie, I have AIDS! It hurts and I'm scared and lonely. I want it all to go away. No one really understands but I know you would. With the exception of my drug abuse and promiscuity (the very things ironically that caused this illness) you understood everything about me. I know you love/loved me.

Mommie, you raised us well. Everyone has rallied and is trying to be supportive. Little Leon, even with his "don't get close to me" attitude, has been caring in his way. Rhea, as always, has presented herself as the most capable of dealing with the situation, but I doubt it very much. I know her a lot better now and I realize what an innocent she is and so sensitive. Keith, ah my Keith. He will cry and hurt most, but he's the one who'll deal with it best. Mommie, Keith, though he doesn't realize it, is the most well-rounded human being of the four of us. Rhea, our baby, will be 29 tomorrow. How about that? She really is beautiful and stubborn, in your kind of way. She's very loving and opinionated. I couldn't have a better sister. I love them all. Linda has been my best friend through all these years. And I wish you could have known Sharon. I can't imagine my life without her. These are my only real friends, outside of the family. I'm so glad I have them all.

Daddy's come a long way. I'm sure there are some things he regrets having said and done. You know he's always been my hero. One step below God, in your eyes and mine. Now, though he's still on a pedestal in my heart, I can actually touch him and feel him holding my hand instead of just a finger.

We are all okay, Mommie, and you can feel very proud. Daddy was an excellent provider, but it was you who raised us and kept our hearts warm. We all love and miss you.

I guess I'll see you sooner. Thanks, I feel better after talking to you.

Love your
Lexi

KECIA LARKIN

CANADA

Kecia is a young Native woman who grew up in a small fishing community on the west coast of Canada. The following is a speech she gave to the Native community in Toronto.

Kecia travels to various Native communities across Canada to tell her story. She has strong views about the connections between problems facing her community — such as sexual abuse, alcoholism, racism — and AIDS. She encourages her community to confront these issues and begin to change.

I grew up in Alert Bay, which is on the northern tip of Vancouver Island. It's a very small isolated fishing community of about 2,500 people. When I was growing up, a lot of things led to my becoming HIV positive. I see and hear about these same things in different communities.

I grew up with alcoholism in my family. I was sexually abused and exploited as a child. These experiences gave me a very distorted view of myself, about who I was and about my life. They basically screwed me up. These things are normal to us on reserves. We breathe them and live them, and sleep with them every night. We pretend bad things aren't happening and that's denial. There are very scary things that I lived through and people I loved went through them, too. I ran away to Vancouver at fifteen to deal with the sexual abuse, hoping that things would get better. But it didn't quite happen that way.

Because I was sexually abused, it was easy for me to become a prostitute. I didn't care about my body anyway, so why not get paid to have sex?

When I hit the streets of Vancouver, I was like a little country bumpkin who just fell off the cabbage truck. I didn't know left from right. I had the knowledge that was given to me as a child, why I bled every month and where babies come from. But you go to Vancouver and there are things like sexually transmitted diseases and AIDS that I didn't know about. It was too embarrassing, too intimate, too touchy to talk about them.

I got a job at the Downtown Eastside Women's Centre and at first I thought I was doing them a big favour by being there. The women told me that they had been raped and they had been hurt and abused. They couldn't deal with it, so they ran away. And then I realized, well geez, they're just like Kecia. She had to run away because she couldn't deal with it.

And nobody was talking about it. I really felt comfortable dealing with these people because they were real. They didn't have anything to hide behind.

The reason I felt safe on Hastings Street was because there were so many people with the same coloured skin as mine — so many people like the people at home. The sexual exploitation, the abuse, the anger, the bitterness, the denial was screaming out every day on Hastings Street. It was just like being at home again, like my little reserve, only in the big city. A lot of kids run away and end up there because they identify with the others, people who've been abused and left home because nobody wanted to talk about it. Because they felt bad for talking about these things. All my life, I'd heard "respect your elders," but they never showed me any respect.

I fell into prostitution, and heroin and cocaine really fast. I was an alcoholic by the age of 15. I felt I had no options. I didn't want to go home and deal with that stuff. I was having fun. I heard about AIDS but I was like everybody else. Oh, it's never going to happen to me so I don't have to worry about it. I figured there was some way to tell by looking if someone was HIV positive.

I found out I was HIV positive after I decided to get off the streets. I met this person who helped me. I didn't know he was from the same background. I knew that he'd been a pimp and a junkie in Toronto. I figured that he was in Vancouver trying to straighten out his life. Just like I wanted to do, but I couldn't, because nobody else wanted to do it with me.

This man contracted the disease in Toronto. Somebody gave it to him. He knew about it, but he didn't tell me. I trusted him, so we never used condoms and we shared needles. He looked healthy. He got into an accident and that's when I found out that he was HIV positive. At that point, I knew that I had it. And then it was easy to blame myself and judge myself because I was just another poor little Indian from Alert Bay who had run away, gotten into drugs and became a prostitute. I felt I deserved it.

When I found out I had it, I said, "Fuck this nonsense! I don't want to deal with this." I pretended it wasn't happening. I felt very dirty inside, very ashamed. I went back to the street, shooting up, sharing needles, working. I didn't care that maybe I was giving this disease to other people the way that I had gotten it. It just didn't seem important because I didn't admit it was happening to me. I was very alone and very afraid. And it's very hard for me to deal with it today because I'm not a murderer. But I see myself that way sometimes when I'm feeling really shitty. I did it because I didn't feel that I had anybody there to support me.

I knew my family was screwed up. I didn't want to go home and say, "Here I am, I've got AIDS, deal with me." Because I thought that they couldn't. I figured they wouldn't welcome me. I kept it a big secret just like all those secrets I kept about sexual abuse. I was taught that you don't talk outside your family anyway, because it's disrespectful, it's wrong. Finally, one day I got really tired. I got really sick. I got really lonely and scared, because I was wired on coke.

I had nowhere to go so I put myself into a detoxification centre. I had to make the hardest decision: whether I was just going to let myself die or whether I would fight. So I phoned my mom and told her where I was. I told her that I was HIV positive. She didn't know what that meant. In small communities, they don't know about it, if they've never had AIDS education. You see it on television − AIDS, AIDS, AIDS − but you change the channel because it's not your problem. That's only in the city.

I explained to my mom what it was. She cried and cried

and I could feel her pain. I was really scared and she was really scared. Somehow we came together and she told me to come home because she needed some help to deal with this. I knew that I did, too, but I was afraid to ask for her help.

I went home and that's where I stayed. If I hadn't, I wouldn't be here talking to you. It scared me to go home, because I didn't know how the rest of my family would react. So we kept it a big secret for a long time since Grandma is pretty judgemental. She likes to criticize.

I didn't talk about this really openly until about eight months ago. My mom disclosed to certain family members that I was HIV positive. I'm really happy and really lucky because I have my family, people who just accept Kecia. I've never really been shown that before. And this is what I'm being shown with my work.

It makes me sad to know there are a lot of people out there who will never have that family support, people who will die alone. I put myself in their predicament and say, "What would it be like if I were alone, if my family had rejected me?" I know that I wouldn't be able to make it alone. I wouldn't be able to sit here and say what I am saying. Because for a lot of us, our families are all we've got.

We all have our little piece of hell, but not enough of us talk about it. It's not just Kecia who has AIDS. There are a lot of things that we need to start working on together.

It's really frustrating because it always comes down to those things that happen: the alcoholism and sexual abuse that nobody wants to talk about. That's why we're running away. That's why we don't want to be at home. That's why we're going out and getting high so we can't feel anything, so we don't have to think about those things. That's why we're not where we're supposed to be. Because of that little piece of hell that we carry around inside that we don't want to talk about because nobody else knows how we're feeling. Yet everybody feels the same way.

We need to talk. We need to yell and scream rather than just sit and suffer in silence, because it's not doing anybody any good. And if anybody's in a position of power, if they're being quiet about these things, it ain't doing their people any good because it's really phoney, it's very fake. And we can see that.

I got into trouble a lot when I was growing up because I have a big mouth. But I love my big mouth. I go to communities to talk about my experiences. I see a lot of people sitting in their chairs, listening to what I have to say. I can feel if it's affecting them to hear me talk about sexual abuse. And I'm not going to stop talking about it.

MARIE WERNER
GERMANY

Marie exchanged many letters with us, but she always stressed the need for anonymity. Like many other contributors to Positive Women, *she is afraid of losing her job if her co-workers and employers were to find out she is HIV positive..Marie was the first woman in Germany to test HIV positive who was not an injection drug user. At the time, she had difficulties with the negative reactions of society to this new disease.*

We asked Marie how she would like to be described in this anthology. This is her reply: "To my mind, this is a difficult question, but perhaps the important factors concerning me are the following ones. Although I don't believe that normal people exist, I am a woman who would be described by others as normal. No exciting details in my life except perhaps my HIV infection. I am working as a scientist at a university. I was a blood donor and so I was tested without knowing anything about it. My boyfriend, whom I knew for about ten years, was bisexual, but I did not know this until after I found out that I was infected. He was a very wonderful man. In 1988, he became ill and in 1989 he died. In the last few years, the themes of my poems have changed towards love, death and my life as an infected woman in a world of men. For me, writing is one of the most wonderful ways to put feelings into reality, and to understand and reflect on what is happening."

Involuntarily in the avant-garde of the women's movement
I am HIV positive
burst open in a domain of men
I am HIV positive
working in a man's profession
I am HIV positive
with men in a bar, taken seriously
I am IIIV positive
with men, morning, noon, evening
I am HIV positive
with men in conversation, the subject of their conversation
I am IIIV positive
Feared of men, accepted, loved
I am HIV positive
free of women, I am alone
with all these men.

*

So you have indeed left me.
Clandestine, quietly, deliberately.
You hardly said a word.
Your apartment remained, the books.
The plants have dried out, you forgot to tell me
I should water them.

So, you went away.
For always, forever.
Without pretending to buy cigarettes,
No indication where,
And I can't even write to you anymore.
There were still a few things to clarify:

What were you thinking of?

So, you went away, you have left me.
Since then I sit in a corner,
Not eating, not answering the telephone.
And you haven't left any explanations for the others.
They don't even ask - what could I say.
Tomorrow I shall plant your grave.

*

Time passes.
Leaves fall to the ground
The sky clear gray in the day.
Early darkness after noon.

The days become shorter
Faces are covered by shadows
Sunshine is replaced by candlelight.
Bare branches everywhere.

The harvest has been gathered.
Remains will rot,
dull green touched with white and frosted grey
There are no flowers left.

It is cold in the darkness.
Ach, if only I could warm you once more
only once again look into your shining,
your sparkling eyes.
Why did you have to go?

*

Dead I shall be.
When the fungi win,
when my courage fails,
when I give up.

Ailing I shall be.
Some time, who knows when,
in the event that it happens to me,
if I cannot manage.

Threatened I am.
Outwardly, the infliction of force,
in the centre, fear and prejudice,
within, my injured will to live.

Fear I have, fear
of being hurt, of hasty words,
of death, slowly dying, of threats,
above all, of myself.

Hard luck I have had, no blame.
Threatened am I, not a threat.
I shall die
and not be dead.

Marie's poems have been translated from the original German.

ELIZABETH
TANZANIA

Elizabeth's story illustrates some of the issues relating to African women and HIV which Rosemary Mulenga from Zambia also raises on page 26. She talks with a critical voice about polygamy, the subservience of women to men, customs surrounding pregnancy, family relations and the hard work of supporting three children while being a single mother with HIV.

Elizabeth works as a nurse in Dar Es Salaam, the capital of Tanzania. She voices her fears about her employer discovering that she is HIV positive. In this respect, she echoes the fears of many HIV positive women employed in all parts of the world.

In a letter to us, Elizabeth describes herself and her reasons for contributing to the anthology: "I am yet another unfortunate woman who has fallen victim to the dreadful AIDS causing virus, HIV. I am 33 years old. I decided to write to you so that I may relate to you my sorrowful story in order for you and me to establish ways and means of helping each other."

After finishing my education and graduating from nursing school, I got married to my long-time boyfriend. This was in 1980. We led a happy married life and we were blessed with two children, a girl and a boy. Although we never quarrelled much, I discovered that my husband was jealous of me. He became suspicious, whenever I came home late from work or from a visit. But anyway, this is usual with lovers. I, on my side, sincerely did not trust him. Because I was his wife and thus under his command, I had nothing much to do other than just cope with the situation. Our customs demand that a wife be faithful to her husband and accept whatever comes from him. Even if it means he comes home one evening in the company of a young lady and proudly announces to you that she – the young lady – will be your co-partner! Some customs are funny, aren't they?

During my third pregnancy, I left for my home in the rural area of Bukoba to prepare for my delivery – this is normal in our customs – where I stayed for more than six months. Later I came back to rejoin my husband in Dar (Dar Es Salaam) and to continue with my job. All those six months I stayed in the rural areas, I never had sexual intercourse with anybody. Did my husband perhaps...?

We went on with life as usual until June 1988, when my husband started complaining of a severe headache. Later he developed fever, night sweats and sudden loss of weight.

After being treated for a long period without genuine recovery, the situation changed. He developed a cough and chest pains. In September 1988, he was admitted to Muhimbili Medical Centre where doctors diagnosed pulmonary tuberculosis. By now, I had started worrying since all the symptoms of AIDS I had heard people talk of were present in my husband. I would have gone on worrying had it not been for the doctor's and nurses' assurance that my husband was suffering from a curable disease.

My relief was interrupted by a sudden haste of my brothers-in-law, who without my consent started making arrangements to have my husband transported home to Bukoba. I got very suspicious and somehow managed to get access to the hospital files. With great shock, I discovered that my husband was suffering from AIDS. To add more fuel to the already over-burning fire, my brothers-in-law started threatening me: that, if in my delay, for I had already cancelled their journey in order to prepare myself, their brother died, then I was to bear the whole responsibility of transporting his remains to Bukoba. I was forced to prepare in great haste, confusion and fears. When I was ready, we left for Bukoba.

In Bukoba, my husband was admitted in Ndologe Hospital where he was to continue with his TB medication. After 60 days of hospitalization, his general condition improved and he was discharged to continue with the remaining medication at home.

I came back to Dar to continue with my job hoping my husband would also join me within a short period of time since he had shown all signs of recovery.

I got the greatest shock of the year when, on March 29, 1990, I got a phone call informing me that my husband had passed away. On further inquiry, I was told that he had been admitted on the previous day after complaining of a severe headache and high fever.

After what had seemed like a century in which I finished all the necessary ceremonials surrounding my husband's death, I once again returned to Dar where I decided to visit a doctor and have myself, as well as my youngest child, tested to ascertain whether or not we had also contracted the disease. On my part, I was almost sure I was positive, for even though people believe in miracles, I didn't consider myself so lucky.

The results were both encouraging as well as shocking. My child was found to be negative, but I was found to be positive.

Well now, my good people, the situation is like this. I have three kids to look after, a very short time to live since I can die at any moment – my husband showed the way – and a lot of errands to run. These errands were not significant when my husband was alive but now, being alone with a family to look after, it has become a real burden. So far I have not experienced any serious ailment. I am also under some traditional medicines. But sometimes I wonder: Does God really exist? Forgive me...

I am still going on with my job as a nurse, which I am sure I might be forced to stop at any moment should my employer find out about my situation. I have so far come across many people who are HIV positive since it is spreading here in our country like bush fire. Whenever we meet, we try to comfort each other and it helps one to cope with the situation and the reality.

HEATHER

CANADA

Heather is a single mother of a young daughter. She formerly ran a daycare centre out of her own home.

There are many important themes in Heather's piece: discrimination, secrecy, sexuality and relationships. For years, Heather told no one that she was HIV positive for fear of losing her job, friends and lovers.

Heather describes her initial overwhelming need to be seen as a healthy person. She discusses what it has meant to her to go from being a person who is HIV positive and healthy to a person who is living with AIDS.

What follows are excerpts from a very long taped interview that Heather sent us.

There was a two-year period when I felt I was healthy and really handling the fact that I was HIV positive. I was functioning normally and pretended it really wasn't there. Though I went to my support meetings, I still felt pretty far removed from people with AIDS. Everything was sort of groovy, so to speak, until I got pneumonia and then the realities of having HIV hit me. Now I must look at it all over again. I went from someone who was HIV positive and healthy to someone with AIDS. That was a big shift. I was really high and positive for a while. But it's difficult to remain positive when you are physically ill.

I didn't tell anyone, except the people I had slept with. Absolutely nobody knew for years until three months ago. My family didn't know. My acquaintances, my friends, people I work with didn't know. It was very alienating keeping it a secret. But when I thought about what would happen if they knew, keeping it a secret seemed less of a stress. My only source of income was running a daycare in my home. And I wasn't willing to deal with what the parents would do if they knew I had AIDS. I was also afraid of losing my childcare licence. This was a very real fear because you can't get insurance when you are HIV positive and you have to have insurance to get a childcare licence.

When I went to the doctor who had given me the HIV test for a physical examination to get my daycare license, she refused to sign the form that I was physically well. I had passed the physical with flying colours, but because of my HIV positive status, she wouldn't sign the form and I got really pissed off.

I went to another doctor, told him I had just moved into town, didn't have a doctor and needed a physical examination to start a job. He did the physical exam including some bloodwork. Everything came back perfectly normal. He signed the form and I was on my way.

So I kept going back to this doctor, because it was really important to me that people see me as someone who is healthy. I even brought my daughter to him. So he became my family doctor, though he didn't even know I was HIV positive.

And then I got this bad cold. I went to my doctor and said, "Look, I have had a cold for two months, and it's getting worse." He said, "Yes, you've got a sinus infection," and gave me some antibiotics. The antibiotics just made me more sick, because the antibiotics tear down your immune system even more. But I still thought it was just a bad cold. I had trouble breathing all night. Next morning I woke up and my lips and my fingernails were blue. I had to breathe really hard in order not to pass out. I called a taxi, went to the hospital and checked myself in. When they examined me, they took a chest x-ray. A doctor who was a respiratory specialist asked me, "Have you ever used intravenous drugs? Have you ever slept with anyone with AIDS? Have you ever been in an accident where you received blood?" And I lied, I was so frightened. I just said, "No, no, no, I'm perfectly healthy." He said, "Look, you have to stay here." My daughter was at daycare. I had no idea I was going to have to stay in the hospital and there were seven kids arriving at the door Monday morning. The shit hit the fan, so to speak, and everything had to come out. I was in hospital for two days before anybody knew. When they found out, everyone just went bonkers. But for me, it was actually a huge release.

*

The truth is having HIV totally screwed up my sex life. The man who was my lover when I found out was absolutely supportive and wonderful. We went on this journey together to find out about AIDS and he really supported me in digging into alternative things, in not buying the doctor's diagnosis, not reading newspapers and staying away from negative stuff. He wasn't afraid of me at all. In fact, I think he should have been more afraid than he was. But it was really good for me to have someone who could make love to me and not be afraid. We started using condoms and he had no problem with condoms. It was fine. In fact we had a lot of fun with them. But for other reasons I broke up with him.

My next lover is the man I am with now. He is really difficult for me to talk about, because I didn't tell him in the beginning. I was so convinced at the point when I met him that I was perfectly healthy, that I couldn't pass the virus to him and that the HIV was nothing. This was when I was really on a roll, very confident, so I didn't tell him that I was HIV positive. I am really sorry now. I know that it was wrong of me to make that kind of decision for him, that I exposed him to the virus without him even knowing about it. For him to expose himself, knowing about it is one thing. But he didn't even have the chance to say no. I wasn't on birth control, so he was very careful because he didn't want me to get pregnant. I essentially practised safe sex with him 99 percent of the time. But there were two nights when we were drunk, came home from a party and screwed on the kitchen table...

When I finally did have intercourse with him on a regular basis, condoms were our form of birth control. I just told him that this is what I use for birth control.

I told him about four months into the relationship. It was really hard and I drove myself nuts knowing that I had to tell him. How do you tell someone that you have knowingly exposed him to AIDS. When I did tell him, I fully expected him to be really angry and to run, and I was ready for that. He pulled away a bit, but mostly he was concerned about me because I was an absolute basketcase. He went to his doctor and was tested. The results came back negative. He waited four or five months and was tested again and he was still negative. So he seems okay.

Since he has known, our sex life has gone downhill. Since I've been sick it's become almost non-existent, because he's afraid of me. He is very wonderful about it, but he's honest. He can't say he is not afraid of me when he is. He has three children and a business and too much to take care of. He was in a bad marriage for nine years.

Sex is slowly phasing out and a good friendship is taking over. That process has been very slow. I know that is what he has wanted for months and I haven't been able to deal with it. He is just taking care of himself. In his head, he has wanted out since I got real sick. He just says, "This is ridiculous, I can't afford to expose myself to this." But his heart goes, "God, that is a real asshole thing to do, to reject someone for their needs."

I answered his ad in the personals — that's how I met him. I was looking for a husband. I wanted to complete my family. I didn't want to be a single parent. I wanted to get married, have a couple more kids, buy a house, do what I had wanted to do in the first place. Since I have been ill, that has fallen by the wayside. It isn't likely that I will have any more kids now, because I'm not willing to deal with what I would have to deal with if my child was born with HIV. I know women who are HIV positive who are having kids. They are willing to deal with it and that's fine. But I know I would not survive losing a baby; it would just absolutely tear me up.

We realize that we are not going to get married and have kids together. We are just in a relationship. We see each other or talk on the phone almost everyday. Our kids spend a lot of time together. I spend a lot of time down at his business and aside from the sex, we're really good friends. We enjoy being with each other.

LINDA ROWE
CANADA

Linda is an AIDS activist and is very public about being a woman living with AIDS.

To understand Linda's poem, it is necessary to know that AIDS is disease which is typically described in stages. "HIV positive" means that a person has been exposed and has produced antibodies to the human immunodeficiency virus (HIV) believed to cause AIDS. During this stage, a person is either asymptomatic (has no symptoms of HIV related illnesses) or is symptomatic (has symptoms of an impaired immune system, but not those symptoms classified as AIDS related complex — otherwise known as ARC — or classified as AIDS. Symptoms of ARC include night sweats, thrush, shingles, etc.)

If a people are diagnosed as having AIDS (in her poem, Linda calls this "full-blown AIDS"), they have one or more of the infections that are recognized by the medical professions as AIDS defining illnesses. These illnesses include pneumocystis carinii pneumonia (PCP), cryptococcal meningitis, etc. Symptoms of AIDS in women have slowly been recognized by healthcare workers and include cervical cancer, pelvic inflammatory disease and other cancers of the reproductive system.

Linda's poem is concerned with the devastating psychological impact of receiving an AIDS diagnosis after being HIV positive for three-and-a-half years.

December 4, 1990

Today, I was diagnosed full-blown
I really, really hurt way down inside.
This is the inside that no one has ever seen
Not even me...
My reality has changed.
In one day I went from well to sick – HIV positive
God gave me 3 1/2 years to accept that I am sick.
What will he give me this time?
He has allowed me one hour to go from sick to dying.
Can the inside be my God?
Does he know how deep my inside is?
Is it possible to share my pain with anyone on this planet?
Can I leave this inside for a while or will it always be
 with me?
Today, I was diagnosed full blown,
I really, really hurt way down inside.
Today... I cried.

CAROLE SNYDER

USA

Carole sent us the following four photographs of farm animals. A former real estate agent, she has recently moved to Seattle from the East Coast.

In a letter to us, Carole gives this information about herself and talks of the importance of her photography to her well being: "Right after I got sick, I felt desolate. I had been a married woman for twenty years. I had two grown daughters and had recently been divorced. So I was just desolate. Then I started becoming more active with my photographs. I would sepia tone them and sell them framed to shops in the city. It was such a joy because I knew that they made people happy and it became one of the biggest things to keep me together during that time."

"Pamela" N.Y.   Snyder '91

"Patti" Romulus N.Y.   Snyder '90

"Nicola & Emma"
Rhinebeck N.Y.   Snyder '91

"Stephanie"
Vieques, Puerto Rico   Snyder '91

JB COLES

USA

JB is a Sioux Indian from South Dakota. Born to a heroin addict and raised in foster care, JB began using alcohol and drugs while still a child. After a three-year stint in the army, she spent several years on the street involved in crime, drugs and religion. JB moved to Alaska and checked into a detoxification centre, hoping to start a new life. It was here that she found out that she was HIV positive.

JB shares her story publicly through newspaper interviews, public speaking and poetry. She wants to let people know what she is going through and to offer her help to others in a similar position.

LIVE

"You Selfish Bastard...

... let me help you live!" he yelled.

The words kept ringing in my ears.

 "Let me help you live!"

I'd never tried that before – life

It was always death and destruction.

Now, for the first time, I'm doing

Something I've Never Done Before.

Most of my "Friends" have left me, But

those who have stayed have truly Been

my life line.

Not only "sharing" my Dis-ease With

them, but life through AIDS.

(By the way, it means And I Deserve Serenity)

More often times than not, in the midst of my anger,

frustration, fear and depression, I'm gently

reminded of why I'm alive, even though it's

hard for me to put into words – I feel it

in my heart.

To be Native, Female and an Alcoholic/

Addict was bad enough – Now I have

AIDS. "How much further Down the Ladder

Can I get?" Yeah, there's no way but up.

I hope for life and all its riches

I live for me and my dog POOH

I pray for Peace and Love

I Do my best to see the bright side

I Grab for the Gusto

My Mother gave me life, but God

gave me Wings, not AIDS.

To Stand Strong and trust in God,

Follow the promptings Within, not Without.
The World is full of Doom and Gloom. I
need not be that way. Living in the Moment
is living Life. One day at a time.
 I shall not die with regrets –
 I shall not die in debt –
 I shall not die alone –
 I will merely pass through a
doorway of such love.

DINA

SWITZERLAND

Dina is a young woman who leads a support group for HIV positive people in St. Gallen, Switzerland. Her piece talks about her relationship with her boyfriend, E, her attempt to kick heroin by using methadone and her support group which has now become an integral part of her life.

We were put in touch with Dina and M (whose work appears on page 89 of this anthology) by Vivi Tobler, Dina's devoted and supportive grandmother. Vivi once facilitated a support group for HIV positive people in Switzerland and carried on an active correspondence with us throughout the initial stages of this anthology. She is the translator of the excerpts from Dina's journal which follow.

DINA

August 14, 1987

Why do you throw shit at me all of the time – as though I were the one who started this whole mess? I want to STOP, stop using my money for dope. It will wreck my body and I will only sink down lower and lower. I cannot stand this life with you any longer, the constant stress, the nervousness and your always making a pig out of me. I do not know why you call me a methadone glutton. Why do you constantly put me down, because I cannot keep my eyes open when I smoke a joint?

Before we went on vacation, I told you that our relationship was not good any more. But you carried on just as though nothing had been said between us. Even with methadone, it takes a lot of will power and self control to keep clean of drugs. I have just come home from work dead tired, and you tempt me with the dope you just brought home! How can I say no? I feel this is the last chance I have to save myself otherwise I will be lost in the quicksand of the drug world.

October 28, 1989

I seem to fly from the heights of happiness into the depths of despair – my moods are like the high waves in the ocean. I do not know if my sadness comes from the love I have for E, whom I just recently met, or does it come from the knowledge that I am HIV positive. The moods come from the innermost part of my being and drown my body and soul. I am so alone and at the same time have the feeling that I am never really capable of being alone. Since I have been living in St. Gall, this is my first real crisis. It started with my pregnancy. The fear that my child could also be positive forced me to have an abortion. I do not want to be sad. I have enough of all these depressions. Yet, I suppose this has to be, for I had to prepare myself for the death of my child.

I saw my baby on the ultrasound! It had legs, little feet, little fingers – everything! I love my baby still to this day. Yes, I would have loved to become a mother, even though I was afraid to lose my freedom and become dependent upon my friend, E. There is no tenderness between us right now and I need his love so much. I feel starved for his love and when he does show me gentleness, the feeling of fear comes again. Is it really genuine or does he feel it is his duty? Oh, please, not that. My pride would break if that were the case. Oh shit, I feel so insecure. I only want to be a self-confident, healthy young woman.

October 29, 1989
We have lost the ability to talk with each other...

October 30, 1989
I sit in the train returning to St. Gall, think, think and think.... At the station I cried and cried. E asked me why – two minutes before the train left – no time and very little trust.

Home again in St. Gall, an evening and night alone in my room.

"Let's spend the night together,
now I need you more than ever!"
My need for drugs has come back, I want to drink all of my methadone at one time, become unconscious – forget.

If our parents do not give us the feeling that we deserve their love and attention, how can we ever believe we have the right to be loved?

November 7, 1989
I am so frightened that the virus has broken out. My lymph

glands are always swollen, I feel weak and tired. When I wake up in the morning, cold perspiration covers my body — I am afraid. Should I tell my boss that I am HIV positive? I just do not know.

November 13, 1989
I still do not feel so well, simply no energy in me any more. Is it the coming of winter that I feel? Despite all this I have the feeling of living intensely. It takes such an effort!

November 29, 1989
I sit now in the train to Zurich and will meet the people of the support group there. Our AIDS Minister, Heiko Sobel, will also join us. We will travel to the Rigi and will stay there in the mountains for four days. E will also come. I look for ward to these days, am actually quite excited. Just think, I can take my dog Nuschka with me. I can hardly live without her at my side. I love her so — she is simply a part of me.

December 1, 1989
The Day of Silence on the Rigi also happens to be E's birth-day!

December 12, 1989
Our feeling for each other is once again a love affair. It is wonderful and since the days on the Rigi, I am even happy once in a while. I feel sheltered and warm when we are together. But today we had some very bad news: we both went to the doctor at the University Hospital in Zurich. The specialist for infectious illnesses told us that E must soon take the antiviral drug AZT. He has a fungus in his mouth and on his tongue. It hurts him terribly when he eats or smokes. I am so afraid for him.

E, you are the most wonderful man I have ever met. I love your eyes when you laugh. They are like stars that lighten your entire face. I love you with all my heart. I will simply not permit you to get sick.

December 13, 1989
I cannot come to a standstill in my inner development or even put in a pause. I feel again as though I were sitting on the top of an enormous wave and being thrown and tossed through life. Every single day is filled with so many experiences that bit by bit I am forced to live a richer and deeper life. Sometimes it is almost too much. I love you, E. Often I try to understand myself and have the greatest trouble analysing my inner being. In spite of all this, I am beginning to like and accept myself. Years ago this would have been inconceivable. I always believed myself to be so bad and worthless. I could never believe that anyone would love me, me just me as I am – Dina!

December 15, 1989
What a wonderful Christmas sermon! A real boost for us all. Too bad that it went by so quickly. I was terribly excited and it was a tremendous test of courage and a confirmation of my own being. E and I had to talk before the congregation of more than a thousand people. We both had to overcome our fears and the stagefright. For the first time, it meant also admitting that we are HIV positive and that we are, despite that, normal human beings. At the end of our little talk, E, with total relief that it was all over, turned to me and gave me a loud smack – this in front of four microphones! This kiss was heard by one thousand members of the congregation.

December 18, 1989

Should I increase my methadone portion? I long to go back to the original portion. I feel so in danger of a return to drugs and think of it at least 20 times each day.

January 2, 1990

I just had a wonderful weekend. Friday evening I went to visit M and we had such a good chat together until two o'clock in the morning. She is a woman in our support group and lives right near us. She is becoming a dear friend to me. I find her a super woman and am so glad that I know her now. On Sunday, E and I, as well as two other people from our group, made a date to go into the woods with our dogs. E was really happy. I have seldom seen him so relaxed and enjoying himself.

January 3, 1990

Total friendship is based on the knowledge of the inner value of the beloved person.

May 1, 1990

Why can I not enjoy fully the fact that I no longer take drugs? Do all the emotions that come in on me disturb my sense of balance?

July 27, 1990

My beloved dog is dead. I am so deeply sad that I feel it in the depths of my stomach. The pain is unbelievable. I would so love to feel her cold wet nose in my hand. She meant so much to me, more than many human beings. Nuschka was the closest and dearest friend that I have ever had at my side. My beloved Nuschka, how I love you and how I wish I could tell you, wherever you are now. My dearest, dearest dog! I miss you so very much. I can hardly endure this sorrow.

Sept. 29, 1990
I still miss you, my beloved Nuschka. I am very very happy though to have Chica, my Bergamasker puppy. But despite Chica, the pain of losing Nuschka is still here whenever I think of her. Generally speaking, my life seems to have taken an upward trend. Like sponges, E and I drink deeply of the love we have for each other. I feel so comfortable now with him. I love you, E, and it is the most beautiful love that I have ever experienced.

M

SWITZERLAND

These are undated excerpts from M's journals over a period of a few years. In them, she sorts through her relationships with various people, her illness as it develops, her addictions, her fear of death, her desire for children and her sense of limited time. She often addresses her husband as "you" in the entries.

M and Dina, whose piece precedes this one, are facilitators of a support group for people living with AIDS and HIV.

M's journal entries have been translated from the original German.

"M"

Drops fall silently on a grey ground
grey on grey in dark shadows
thoughts circle silently in an abysmal heart
empty and lonely in dark shadows
screams cry silent in a far distance
no one picks them up
silent, completely silent, falling into dark shadow

*

Self pity, fear is slowly gnawing at me. AIDS – is it true that a time bomb ticks within me? How long until this new, frightful epidemic breaks out within me? How long until my body has no more resistance and slowly but surely disintegrates? How long until my last hour strikes? Should I prepare myself for death?

Oh God, I have lied to everyone in Zurich. I am so afraid of being treated like a pariah, and HIV positive people are being treated that way. What will become of me? I am 25 years old, a grown-up woman, you would think. But look at me, what am I? A nothing, a nobody. It is so terrible.

*

My sister really hurt me, as she has done several times before. Not only has she gone completely mad concerning AIDS, but our relationship isn't progressing positively at all. Our, or rather my, childhood emotions are so strong, so sore; it hurts me still so very much. Well, it's a pity that I can't tell her the truth, but she would avoid me like the plague.

AIDS at times hounds me with fear, but the panic in my case is out of place – when you catch it, you've caught it. I've been feeling healthy, and the HIV antibody is not AIDS as yet.

How many people get sick, suffer, die, and I feel content?

*

Time flies so quickly, it almost frightens me. Who knows how much longer I will live? Who knows how much longer I can be with you? I should begin to make each day beautiful, as if it were the last one. Perhaps it will come soon, my last healthy day. Nevertheless, I want to be an optimist. Perhaps I will remain healthy. I am tough. Perhaps I will be lucky.

*

Naturally I ask myself at times if I want to have children. I ask myself often. And I know it is not a real question in my situation. Sometimes this hurts. Perhaps it would be beautiful to create a large family. Well, what does it matter? This way is also good. Aren't there already enough kids in this shitty world which gets increasingly worse?

*

Sometimes, I hear it quietly within me, my timebomb, tic-toc-tic-toc. I don't know whether it is my imagination, at moments when I feel like I do now. I feel alone and forlorn. I feel like lying in bed with a good book that steers one's attention away from reality. I don't have one. It's snowing again, quite gently. No sun in view, no warmth.

W comes to mind, a sad story. He got married because his wife had cancer and was going to die soon. She wanted to die with his name. And he is now dead himself, hanged in a cell. Sometimes, I see this picture before me. Must I die soon, too?

You were always afraid of this sickness, K. I remember clearly when we read about it for the first time. I wasn't preoccupied by it, I smiled about it and couldn't take it quite seriously. Both of us caught it and still so many others, and who will die of it nobody knows.

*

I saw a film yesterday on TV about a gay AIDS case. A real American-style film, but it hit home. Imagine, a few times tears came into my eyes! And today I thought a great deal about AIDS. There are so many questions, so much fear which I repress quite well. Sometimes, it seems to me, I can cope with it. In any case, the fear harms me. I don't want to harm myself any more. I have enough problems already, more tangible ones.

Well, I don't really know how I can cope with this, but I simply must. I want to live some more.

*

I simply had no inclination to go to the O's. I sense how my relationship with them is somehow odd, because they know — that's inhibiting somehow. Last time, we didn't even exchange a kiss. I don't know whether fear is behind it, or just insecurity. For my part, I feel insecure about them. I never quite know how close, for example, I can come to the children. Well, I must simply learn how to deal with all of this. But quite often I feel fear. It is simply depressing to know that a timebomb ticks within me.

*

Can you imagine how it is when you have fear, really deep fear, because you don't know how sick you are or whether the doctor is about to give you a death sentence? Sometimes I sit here at home by myself, feeling utterly alone and isolated with my fear. Nobody is here to whom I could openly talk about this. There is something wrong here, somehow there is something wrong with my body, in my belly. I feel this, and now I have found enough nerve to go to the doctor after more than three months of this.

*

Well, I don't have much time to live anymore. It will just be a matter of time before my sickness begins. Or, perhaps it has started already? Do I really have pneumonia? Well, this will soon become apparent.

I don't feel well. I am sad. All my hope is destroyed. I will have to leave my job. Will my travel plans not happen either? Now that I have decided to travel two months after you've left, I am afraid. When I get sick, when I am despairing, who will be here to embrace me, to comfort me?

*

I must concretely begin to come to terms with my life and my death.

My last period of life has begun, my old age, the evening of life. And for all that, I am only 27 years old and have not yet lost my will to live. The virus in my blood, which increases and attacks my helper cells, weakens my immune system. And now, pneumonia. I am truly afraid for my future.

I must go to the hospital for tests. I should be there for two days. That alone can throw me into a panic-like fear. I couldn't sleep last night, talked for a long time with F. That did me good. Simply to talk and to listen about life, love, problems, and whatever. I finally did sleep for two hours. I

94

don't feel terribly unwell. Above all, I will never lose my optimism and my hope.

*

Feeling better, I am even going to work again today. Much has happened to my life in the past few days. I cannot do a thing except attempt to be strong, courageous and optimistic. Next week I will most likely start the anti-viral drug AZT. Then I might remain well a bit longer and live longer too. I find it difficult to write down my thoughts, and to allow my feelings to surface.

Today we have been married one year and eight months. That is beautiful. And still I can say with my whole being I truly love you. And there are moments, right now for example, when I am truly happy. I say this because I often think that perhaps I don't have much longer to live. Being happy is always just moments in life which arrive independent of whether you have sorrow or whether your life bears the stamp of misfortune.

*

B died about a month ago of AIDS. Ach, what can I think about it? B was once a blonde angel. I don't want to think anything.

*

My lungs have been hurting me all the time for a week. Damn, today I must tell this to the doctor. I know I should not smoke anymore, but I cannot stop. Sometimes fear rises within me. How much longer until the next damn sickness comes? People are dying. When is it my turn?

*

Surely V has his child by now. Small children affect me most strongly. They affect me because I like them. They are such helpless creatures and yet so natural and so strong. Children have life before them. What kind of life will they have? What will the world look like in a few years when I am not around anymore? Would we have a child, or two, if I were well? Ach, sometimes it is hard.

*

And now I must simply learn to live with it. Pneumonia, shingles, thrush, tablets, controls, fear and tears. How hard must my illness be for you, and then my death? You too must learn to handle this. I wish both of us a truly beautiful birthday evening. You too are now 27 years old. Time passes and we are always getting older.

*

I believe I have not ever cried as much as I have in the past few days. It is cruel to constantly have these pains and not be able to do anything about it. Well, that's how it goes with me. After the pneumonia, shingles, what will come next? Soon I won't be able to think of anything else. The pain literally eats me up. Today I had a strong desire to take something, simply so that it stops hurting.

*

I'm not in a good mood. It is really shitty sometimes. Outside, damn pissy weather. I am always in pain and slowly

I am becoming sick of everything. It is again the 13th. Now it is 21 months since we got married. One year and nine months and soon it will be three years that we have been together. I still love you. I would never share you with another woman. Soon it will be Christmas once again. I find it a sad time because so many people become aware of their solitude. I am not lonely, but sad nevertheless. How much longer will I live? How much longer will I remain fairly healthy? And how long will my sickness torture me? I will never have children. To see children hurts me and makes me sad. Yet there is nothing more beautiful than to see laughing, happy children. You would surely be a good father.

After I'm gone will you one day have children?

*

My little sister called me yesterday. She was very nice. I always fear that my friends will not like me anymore once they know ....

Shit! Sometimes I feel so terribly stupid and boring. I console myself that I have experienced other things, had other experiences in my life and that I must fight an illness which requires an energy and a strength which perhaps many other people don't have.

I often feel totally happy as well. I am still healthy, can experience so many beautiful things.

*

Today is my last day of AZT. It seems strange. It is already half a year since I began my treatment and since the pneumonia. And I have recuperated so well in this time. I only hope this five week break will not harm me. But it is not that long.

I am wondering how much of it is all in my mind. Surely that matters too. I do not want to get sick and I must not. I have so much more before me. I am still young and maybe, who knows, I might still conceive a child. But seriously, don't hold on to any illusions. That would be quite unlikely.

Drinking coffee, it tastes so good. Again, I am completely enjoying the morning. How can one do otherwise when all is so beautiful around me? Ach, sometimes I am truly grateful that I can experience such moments.

*

Again a cigarette, although I should really not smoke so much, damn it. I did ten bends and ten push-ups and was panting like an old woman. My lungs are really bad. Well, I am an old woman. Soon I will have my birthday and will be 28 years old. Will I succeed and reach 30?

*

I dreamt I was pregnant and would have a child and there was no risk involved. But, this dream is a dream. Sometime, when some cure is found, I will be too old. One can arrange life for oneself without children. But then, I am optimistic about my personal life and that is almost worth more, isn't it?

*

I am sick again, probably pneumonia. Must swallow antibiotics in large quantities. Shit, how much I hate these white things which I can hardly swallow. Today I feel better. In any case, I can again breathe more easily.

*

Through the self-help group I have met a few new people. Somehow there is another type of understanding in a friendship when one knows certain things about the other. Openness is good, though not all the time. I am much better again. Now I hope to have some quiet time. Not to be well takes so much energy, which I could use elsewhere.

I went to the doctor today. I am really curious about my test results. If it is "the" pneumonia – and I simply do not believe it is – that would mean that I have AIDS. I am also curious about my blood counts. Now, after a break of approximately three weeks I must start AZT again. Again four tablets daily.

*

How often I am still able to repress this sickness. Simply to act as if it doesn't exist, as if it weren't here, neither the fear of suffering, the loneliness and death. I have you and how glad I am, how unspeakably relieved that I have one person who truly stands by me, truly is with me. But I should treat this relationship carefully. We are free people and nobody is obliged to stay with the other, even though sickness and death is near. Relationships cannot be built and maintained through pity and force. Everyone is free to go. How much I feared that you would leave me and I would suddenly be alone without you, you who give me all the strength and the courage to survive. No, I will try to treat you how I wish you would treat me: with respect, without force, loving and not possessive. You are not my possession, as I am not yours.

I have two people in this world who I am certain will stay with me whatever happens, who will stay with me till death. You and my mother. What would I be like without you?

Would I be off drugs, like I am now, to some extent a competent person? How do other people manage who do not have the luck to have people around them to share life with them, a threatened life even, as mine is.

I don't know to what extent I have come to terms with sickness and death. I know only what damn fears I had when I had the first bout of pneumonia and the shingles. Now things are going well with me. I swallow my AZT four times a day without hesitation. I do not create so many fears, let them get me down. But is this right? Is this self-protection from despair? Does one need this in order to be able to live? I don't know. And when the day arrives and somehow I believe that it will come, how will I stand then?

*

What can one make out of one's life? Most people at our age are established, have children by now, family. But we, who can't have children — which perhaps is good — must look for other ways, must set other goals, must find other experiences and meanings.

JAE
USA

JAE is a native New Yorker, currently living in Seattle, Washington. She has a degree in creative writing and women's studies and is presently pursuing a masters degree in social work.

JAE takes up the theme of sex addiction in her writing. This theme is one which is discussed in the gay community, particularly since the advent of AIDS, but not often mentioned by women. JAE relates her sex addiction and her HIV status to an attraction to death. She also believes that both addiction and HIV represent a search for the spiritual.

JAE is bisexual, so she fits neither into the lesbian nor into the straight communities where sexual identity and preference are more regimented. The lack of acceptance of her bisexuality has, she believes, forced her "into the closet" and she is similarly closeted about being HIV positive.

At the end of her article, JAE talks about the difficulties in practising safer sex. Some explanation might be required here. She mentions dental dams which are squares of latex, originally used in dental surgery and now less successfully in oral sex. Nonoxynol-9 is a spermicide which has anti-HIV properties. Rubber gloves are used to prevent contact with vaginal fluids.

JAE's collage follows on page 107 and two photographs of her "found images" (urban graffitti about AIDS) appear on pages 132 and 225.

Angry, yes, I was angry and I still get angry. First I experienced the shock of the HIV positive result. But the shock wore off in a wave of realizations over a period of weeks. Most of all, I realized I had sexualized my existence as a female. I had been aware of my sex addiction for a few years and had been dealing with my compulsive sexual behaviour with a limited success rate. This final shock hit me like a lightning bolt and has dramatically changed behaviours I have struggled with for over 20 years.

My anger is mostly directed at myself, at my naiveté, at my blinders. I have lived as a sexual creature of luck. I simply believed I was lucky; I have attributed many incidents in my life to luck. This belief blinded me to the fact that I could get AIDS. I foolishly thought I was immune. I was living out an adolescent fairy tale, acting out, not thinking I could get caught. I was doubly addicted: I was smoking pot and having sexual affairs. They fit together well. It was a delusional existence.

Nothing is worth getting AIDS. Friends whom I have told I was a sex addict made light of it. In 1988, I learned a lot more about addiction. I learned the definition of addiction is the steady movement toward death. One friend to whom I told this said, "Sex is healthy. How can it lead to death?" I had just finished a bout of doctor visits which finally diagnosed my female problems as the sexually transmitted disease, chlamydia. I told her having sex without protection can lead to death. Yet did I practise what I knew? The answer is obvious.

I have found myself in the position of having to explain sex addiction to people unfamiliar with the concept. Like any addiction, it is a compulsion that consumes the major part of one's life, devouring time with the surrounding rituals. It is an escape from pain. I also believe it is a search for the spiritual. Sex addiction for me was the inability to say no, the craving of attention, the denial that my body, my relationships and my career were suffering. It is a hard addiction to identify, because, like eating, it is an integral component of our lives and so it often goes unrecognized. Very often sex addicts are filled with the shame of secret drives and behaviours they cannot talk about, let alone acknowledge. Many women are readily able to identify as love addicts, or as co-dependents which is considered more acceptable.

Now, to a large degree I am silent about my HIV status. I am living in a closet which is not unusual for me. I have lived in closets before: I have crossed racial and gender barriers. I am bisexual, a controversial word in the lesbian community and an obscured position in the heterosexual world. I learned it was best not to mention my bisexuality with my lesbian friends, and my relationships with black men with my family.

When in a steady relationship, my sexual addiction has been in the form of insisting on an open relationship in which I have had sexual affairs. I have strived to be open. I have investigated group marriage and polyfidelity. But even that seemed too closed to what I valued as my freedom to be sexually active. What has all this sexual freedom brought me? First, a distraction from developing other aspects of myself, and second the worst new plague of our times. I have focused on one part of me, my sexuality, to the detriment of other parts.

My beliefs about sexual freedom have centred around several core archetypes. The major one is that of the sacred prostitute who is the fire keeper for the Goddess. She is not tied to any one man but offers herself as a gift and healer. The healing comes through her sexuality. I have also been a believer in serial relationships as the norm of the female evolutionary process.

I never felt I fit into the roles for women that our society dictates. I have tried to live a new sexual freedom and found myself trapped in it. What is true here? These theories resonate within me, but I am using them as excuses for behaviours that were not always appropriate. This is where my addiction lies. I was being true to myself and yet I did not know what that was.

I have hit bottom in what I have come to know as my sex addiction, but it is an uphill climb from here. I am asymptomatic. I am in a positive mind frame. I have discovered my positive status early. I believe I will have many years of good health. I am re-examining my belief in luck and my resources of responsibility and finally balancing the two. I am moving in and out of denial, in and out of anger, in and out of the frustration of what it means to be a woman with AIDS in today's world. I am trying to balance awareness and knowledge, so I do not get lost in the denial stage of this grieving process. I feel good about the path I am on now. I have given up all addictions except sugar. I am often physically tired, but I work 40 hours a week. I am in a Master's Program. And I am cleaning out the residues of 15 years of marijuana in my body. I am moving on with my life while I can.

It figures I would get AIDS. This is my first step in processing the anger, in accepting that I have this virus in my body, and that in some ironic way it makes sense. I have always stood on the opposite side, on the minority side. Politicians I vote for lose elections. I join thousands of people at peace rallies, women's rights marches and gay pride celebrations, but we are not the people represented in our American culture. We have a current president who says the peace movement is dead. We go to war to police countries in

my name but I do not agree. I am overshadowed, outnum-
bered, a worker without a voice that is heard. I have been
angry a long time. I wrote poetry, studying with Audre
Lorde, to express this anger and frustration.

Here it is again like a slap in the face: I am different. My
anger is justified. When will it end? When I die, I guess. I
am going on forty and I am living every minute. I have got to
get over this anger, let go of my frustration, in order to stay
healthy. I do have hope despite my fears.

I believe in luck and I also believe the flip side of luck is
responsibility. As I said before, I should have known the risks
I was taking. After all, I attended ACT-UP meetings in New
York. I knew the statistics. I had friends practising safer sex
and talking abut it. I was reading the PWA Coalition
Newsletter and other AIDS-related literature. I know I am
responsible and would have been more so sexually if I had not
been in my addiction.

I have been in the grieving process, grieving for my sexuality and for my life before the virus entered my body. But
even with this virus, life goes on and I can even welcome the
changes that have been forced on my behaviour. I am now a
sex addict serious about recovery. I am looking for new archetypes and new images for women's sexuality. I am re-examining those we already have and searching within myself for
healthy balances.

My sex life is now latex, bubblegum flavoured dental
dams, nonoxynol-9, rubber gloves. It is not so frequent and
with one partner who loves me despite it all. The strain and
stress on this relationship has stretched us to the limits of caring and growth. Yes, I am lucky and I have finally taken
responsibility in this arena of my life.

My sexual search has been a spiritual longing and this foreign HIV virus is steering me on my path to discover a new

self, a new way of partnership. Perhaps a new archetype of women's sexuality will form in my process of discovery and recovery.

– JAE

107

IRIS DE LA CRUZ
USA

September 20, 1953 - May 11, 1991

*After Iris' death in May 1991, her mother, who sup-
ported her throughout her illness, wrote the following
tribute to her daughter in the July issue of the* PWA
Coalition Newsline*., a monthly publication of the*
People with AIDS Coalition of New York, *where
Iris had a regular column called "Kool AIDS": "Your
days were filled to capacity. You bounced from work, to*
GMHC *(Gay Men's Health Crisis) for lunch, gossip,
acupuncture and workout in the gym, to the Center for
a talk with your friend Barbara, to your group, to your
therapist, and then home. You took over my house and
my heart.... I will remember Iris De La Cruz with her
long red nails, her skinny pants, her long pony tail
with big bows in her hair and her infectious laugh.
Whenever I came to you with small problems, you would
listen and then very simply you would say, 'Mom, in
the great big scheme of things in life, who gives a fuck?'
You know what? She was right."*

*The following piece was first published in Iris de la
Cruz's column in the October and November 1990 issues
of* PWA Coalition Newsline.

INVASION OF THE PATIENTS FROM HELL
AT NEW YORK UNIVERSITY HOSPITAL
or
HOW I SPENT MY SUMMER VACATION

I'm a true believer in the concept of "if you ignore it, it'll go away" which is probably why I have AIDS right now (as opposed to simply being HIV positive). Anyway, about a year ago, I got into this whole work-out regimen, trying to change my body image from piglet to an American gladiator. And it was going along pretty well. But then something truly amazing began to happen. My belly started growing and I'd work out even harder. I thought it was gas and, try as I did, farting just wasn't making it go down. I began to suspect that nobody gets gas for a year running without ever relieving it.

It finally got to the point where my boyfriend was getting these goofy looks from people in the street (the kind reserved for expectant parents) and the pain was getting excruciating. In what appeared to be my eighth month, I went into the hospital.

New York University Hospital has two parts, the regular hospital building and the Co-op that's basically set up like a medical Howard Johnson's. I got stuck in the regular hospital building waiting for a bed in Co-op care. Big mistake. I had a private room and spent most of my time tearing down the precautions sign. And I got to meet some very interesting people (more on that later). Finally, I noticed that I was getting my meals (ha-ha) on paper plates. And nobody else was. DISCRIMINATION. Wait'll ACT-UP hears about this! I tore up the nursing station. I have a history of TB (three years ago) and nobody thought to put in the record that it had been treated. They checked it out and gave me regular plates. And took me out of my private room. My new roommate was a

Hasidic Jew who really was very sweet but I don't know if she was ready for me or my pals.

Let's talk about the interesting people. To be fair, I have a personal problem with anyone whose sole occupation is to fix up other peoples' lives. We are talking about the wanna-be psychiatrists known as social workers. A lot of my good friends are social workers, so I imagine most of them are good, concerned people. It's just that somehow I keep running into marshmallow minds. I hate being in bed for anything more than six hours. Except if I have company. And to be perfectly honest, a week in the hospital was making me a mega-bitch. Finally, after all my bitching and hostility, they sent in a social worker to see about hooking me up to Co-op care. I wasn't real impressed with her (to be honest, she turned me right the fuck off) but I was desperate. After about six more days of the staff treating me like a demented person that needed to be handled with kid gloves, I got my marching orders. But before that, I read my charts and apparently Little Miss Social Worker was as taken with me as I was with her. The following is a direct quote, taken from my charts: "She appears not to accept the potential seriousness of her condition — using total denial and externalizing her problems." Miss Rubin, you have an open invitation to sit in on the support group I facilitate or any of the AIDS training sessions I do. With social workers. Doncha just love perceptive people?

I moved to the Co-op. Heaven! No more nurses popping in and out of my room screaming about my smoking and oxygen tanks. Privacy! And most of all, the chance to wear street clothes and be around other people living with AIDS. Best of all, it gave me a chance to sneak out and to be alone with my boyfriend Paul.

My family has always been very supportive throughout

my illness, which is probably why I'm still here. My mom would come to the hospital and then go to work. (Alright mom, are you happy now? She's always telling me I'm ungrateful.) My brother Randy made sure I was aware of the fact that I had a "cartoon body." What immediately came to mind was those cartoon dots with circle bodies and stick figure arms and legs. How sexy. But Paul was very patient, spending nights holding me and not doing anything more than touching and reassuring me. Amazing, since this is a relatively new relationship. At Co-op you're supposed to have a care-partner stay in your room with you.

I learned a lot of things with my gut all bloated. Number one was I gave up any illusions of ever trying to look cute in maternity clothes and I realized baggy tee-shirts and spandex pants hide a multitude of body flaws. Did you ever see a fat couple with big guts walk down the streets? I always wondered how they fucked. Well, let me tell you it must be with great difficulty. Paul has a bit of a belly and a simple hug became an exercise in acrobatics and manipulation.

The first thing I did at the Co-op was to go down to the smoking lounge and see who I knew there. The Co-op has a large percentage of people living with AIDS, much to the dismay of all the old men there for prostate surgery. Come to think of it, they could have been my brothers, since we shared similar body contours.

Well, low and behold! The guys hanging out read like a Who's Who of the HIV community. Sitting in the middle of all the madness, holding court, was my very own Newsline editor, Phil. And he was surrounded by some very impressive people, like the activists Vito Russo and Damien Martin and some other guys that aren't gonna talk to me 'cause I didn't mention them here. Anyway, I sat down and we had warm and touching conversations about the butts of men walking past and who was fucking whom in the real world. Paul came by in the middle of all this and sat silent with his mouth hanging open. But I have to hand it to him, he was cool. He laughed at all the right moments, even though I don't know if he ever really appreciated the humour. I felt like Wendy and the Lost Boys from Peter Pan.

Finally weeks and weeks went by and I saw all my pals leave, one at a time, until I was basically alone. Phil kept calling and coming by and was really very loving to me. But I had to make new friends and come up with new and improved ways to keep myself amused. You would have felt I was in a hospital or something. I made friends with the cutest couple, John and his lover.

Finally, when I was about to scream behind the decor and the ever-expanding size of my stomach, I came up with the brilliant idea to redecorate. So, in the middle of the night, when most of the staff was chillin' out, I dragged Paul up to the medical floor. There we proceeded to decorate all the IV poles with pink ribbons and balloons. Everyone woke up to party IVs, and the nurses, who were real cool anyway, thanked us. We were approaching week five in the hospital.

By this time, the pain was becoming unbearable and my stomach was gross. The sonogram showed two masses in my ovaries and they started talking heavy hysterectomy action. Gilda Radner move over. Dreams of rotten malignant tissues filtered through my mind. Paul would hold me at night 'cause I'd be crying in my sleep.

I had been in the hospital for five weeks and my stomach was looking more and more obscene in its sheer size. The decision to do a hysterectomy had been made and the gynaecologist who was supposed to perform the operation had me on antibiotics in a last ditch effort to see if I'd respond. When it became apparent that I wasn't responding and this guy wasn't giving any specific dates to operate, my primary care physician called me into his office. The decision to go ahead and have a hysterectomy was by no means an easy one for me to make. Visions of spending my life bearded and titless flittered through my mind. Also, my female organs were a PART OF ME! For all the pain and aggravation, I came into this world with them and I wanted to leave in much the same manner. And my body, between having AIDS and having spent my life as a street warrior, already had various ugly little scars and stretch marks. Any plans to do nude modelling were dashed years ago, but this sort of put a cap on it.

So I was with my doctor in his office and he was livid. I had never ever seen him so upset and I'm quietly trying to remember who on staff I'd insulted this time. "Do you know what the expression 'jerked around' means?" he asked. It seems the gynaecologist, who was also a friend of my doctor, was procrastinating and real content to just let me hang around the hospital *ad infinitum* without ever doing the operation. After calling this guy all sorts of pussies and basically going off, my doctor promised to find someone qualified to do the operation. My initial reaction was one of feeling guilty for having put my doctor through all this. I tried to be very level-headed and comforting, saying it really didn't matter. I had to sneak out and run my Friday night HIV group, so I really didn't have time to examine the ramifications of what all this really meant. I had brought this up in the group without really dealing with it, sort of as a political issue. I really don't like using my group for myself. I have a therapist and a great support system. The group is really for group members. Maybe I just have to get over this, but I have a problem when facilitators hog up groups all the time with their own personal shit. So I did the group and snuck back into the hospital. Afterwards I found myself alone in my room. Finally, I began to realize the ramifications of what was happening.

Approximately seven years ago, I wound up in Harlem Hospital being treated for pelvic inflammatory disease (PID). It came out of nowhere. Basically, one day I was fine and the next day I was being admitted through emergency with fevers and unimaginable cramps. At first I had thought the pain was due to constipation. That's not far off since opiates are real constipating. And I had been taking methadone and shooting dope. My boyfriend would bring me up a couple of bags in the hospital and I ran it through the IV line. (I was considering leaving the line in when I left the hospital. No more hunting for veins.) Since I was receiving methadone in the hospital, they were aware of the fact that I was an addict. No one ever suggested HIV testing. This was seven years ago. The PID was treated, I recovered and went about my business, thinking it was a freak occurrence since I had no history of sexually transmitted diseases or gynaecological problems.

Alone at night (doesn't the shit always hit you at night?) feelings that I thought were resolved hit me like a building falling on me. I remember when I was newly diagnosed with AIDS I would ride the trains and have thoughts like, "Would these people still be riding with me if they knew I had AIDS?" And I'd see couples and families and get very depressed thinking that this part of my life was over. I'd feel so dirty. I felt I was the only woman in the world with this virus and was judged to be unclean every time I walked into a doctor's office. I went through a period of wanting my own eating utensils and being real uptight about sharing bathrooms. I felt there was a big scarlet letter A on my forehead and everyone who was near me knew I had AIDS. I was therefore unclean and not worthy to share even the air. I wanted to die.

I had worked so hard. I had already been drug-free when I was diagnosed and I busted my ass with my therapist dealing with all the negative emotions that came with having AIDS. And I had come so far. Far enough to where I was counselling other people dealing with AIDS. And now this doctor was dancing around, willing to let me die because my body was putrid. My blood was tainted and filthy and carried death. And I had no anger towards this man! It was all directed inward at myself. I went into a depression and refused to eat or go for my medications. I spoke to no one.

The staff at NYU Co-op care is amazing. My doctor (who doesn't want to be mentioned by name) found himself many times in the position of a therapist. Finally, after I refused medication for the umpteenth time, one of the nurses spoke to me. Everything came out. I knew from experience that hospital staff gossip. Every time I'd go for my meds, I felt like staff all knew that this guy refused to operate because I was dirty. The nurse's name was Diane DiBernardo and she didn't take no shit. I probably recovered because she was there. She treated me as an equal with some medical knowledge and spent time kicking it with me, like any other woman. Yo Diane, I owe you.

I also had a lot of support from my friends and family. Phil, our friendly *Newsline* editor, was with me all the way, as was my therapist and boyfriend. Love truly does heal.

Finally the chief resident operated himself. My doctor scrubbed up and assisted in the operation and the surgery went well. I'm back at work, went to Washington yesterday with ACT-UP for benefits for women with PID, and am generally acting crazy again. The sad fact is that I should have been tested seven years ago for HIV. And the infection that I had been complaining about for almost two years prior to the hysterectomy should have been addressed. Doctors should really examine the reasons why they entered the "healing art" of medicine and maybe read the Hippocratic Oath once in a while. And women shouldn't be getting sick and left to die because there is no research on women and HIV. Our women are dying untreated and without benefits because, although sero-positive, PID is not considered an opportunistic infection by the Center for Disease Control. Women are going untreated because they can't afford what little treatment there is. As women are the caregivers, if we allow our women to die, we are also condemning society to the same fate.

My feeling is that I didn't have to develop AIDS and the hysterectomy was preventable. I still can't find out if the ovarian abscesses were due to AIDS or just "women's problems." And yeah, I'm angry. Blood is dripping from my eyes. But I guess that's why we have ACT-UP. The depression is gone. But the other day, I was with my friend Lydia and we talked about having babies. And it had struck me that even if there's a cure for AIDS tomorrow, I could never have another baby. There is a part of me gone forever and I'm still in mourning for it.

SUSAN

USA

Susan is married and the mother of two teenaged children. She lives in New Hampshire. For many years, Susan was a teacher, but today she is no longer able to work at this job. Instead, she does a lot of public speaking about living with AIDS to schools and community groups. At the request of her children, she limits her public speaking to groups outside her local community in order to protect their privacy.

Susan calls herself a compulsive journal writer. The poem she submitted to Positive Women *is a nurturer's commentary on AIDS.*

The summer I first developed "symptoms"
I began what I called my "June Cleaver psychosis."
On good days, inviting a multitude of kids in
For sandwiches and cookies
Tempted to believe that
A shirtwaist dress and apron and the preparation of food
Might ward off the virus like a cross does a vampire.

At Hanukah, the following winter
As blood counts dwindled and surgery loomed closer
I invited a family of six, at the last minute, for potato latkes
Relishing the anxiety of not being able to grate enough potatoes in time
I magically produced the golden latkes
A good stand-in for the blood platelets I was unable to maintain.

This week, when a friend was sick and dying
And my own fear filled me with helplessness
At seven one morning
I prepared a pot of chicken soup to deliver
Believing that it contained the healing rituals passed on to me
By my mother and grandmother
The joy of feeding so genetically a part of me
More potent than any stress management activity.

I have an on-going fantasy
That someday the *New England Journal of Medicine*
Will publish an article about "phase 3 testing"
Showing "promising results" both anti-viral and immune boosting
From warm chocolate chip cookies

Fresh out of the oven
Chocolate melting on the tongue like holy-wafers
Out performing AZT and pentamadine
Brimming with non-toxicity
and sweetness
and joy
And "irrefutable clinical evidence"
That these cookies can immobilize the virus
And restore the T cell counts to normal levels.

DARLENE DEVOS

CANADA

Darlene lives in rural Ontario, where she has lived a physically active life in the countryside, working with animals.

Of the many poems that Darlene sent to us, we selected three that address very different issues. In the first poem, Darlene speaks of the awkwardness of practising safer sex as a lesbian. The second poem, written at Christmas time, describes her depression while she was hospitalized for cytomegalovirus (CMV). This AIDS-defining infection often leads to blindness. Darlene's final poem conveys her general sense of alienation.

LESBIAN, LOVE AND AIDS

Rubber gloves
Condom tongues
its plastic touch
barriers that
make it mean so much

Rubber walls
inside my mind
not knowing to reflect or rebound
my only input consists of sound

Its all so new, this way to screw
Living in a respectable head
Learning to make a new bed
A new way to be clean
have hygiene
and be safe
To make this world
a better place

*

TORONTO GENERAL HOSPITAL'S NIGHTMARE

They say I've got CMV of the retina
and esophagus
I'm treated for that and I'm constantly
nauseous
I'm in such a desperate need to have
a break

Because no more of this my nerves
can take
It doesn't feel like Christmas to me
at all
When I hear all the nurses out in
the hall
laughing and joking and feeling
quite high
and all I want to do is sit down
and cry
I'm just getting more and more deeply
depressed
My life has never been such a
mess
I've never been so sad in my life
I can't live any more in this kind
of strife
I'm leaving tomorrow, someone's coming
to see me
and like it or not I'm pulling my IV
I need at least one day to be free
Never had so many needles sticking
in me
I'm going to go crazy if I stay any
longer
I'm losing my mind, it's making me
bonkers
I know when I'm out and I've cleared
my head
I'll stop wanting to feel like I'd
rather be dead

*

A pure white room
my heart is beating
Watching the flies
mating on the ceiling
It gives me such a weird
and eerie feeling
The crawling growths
that cause insanity
And the fear of constant
rejecting
humanity.

KIMBERLY AND MEGHAN
RICHARTZ
USA

Kimberly writes: "I am 24 years old. I have been married for three-and-a-half years. My husband Joel and I have a two-and-a-half-year-old daughter. Our daughter's name is Meghan Ruby Richartz and she is our beautiful gift from God. My family found out that we were both infected with the AIDS virus in December of 1989. My husband is HIV negative. Meghan and I are both symptomatic and on various medications. For the last 14 months, I have been praying and begging to be awakened from this terrifying nightmare."

Kimberly sent us this photo of herself and Meghan, as well as a finger-painting created by Meghan.

KIMBERLY RICHARTZ & MEGHAN RUBY RICHARTZ
JANUARY 1991

Meghan Richartz
2/1990 age 2½

ISABEL

ZIMBABWE

Isabel is a white woman who lives in Zimbabwe. It is interesting to compare and contrast her concerns with those of Dambudzo, a black Zimbabwean woman whose work appears on page 168 in this anthology.

Isabel's piece records her process of coming to terms with the changed relationship between herself and her partner when they suddenly found out without preparation that they were both HIV positive. She feels that this experience has brought them closer together.

In spite of pressure from society to give up hope of having a child, Isabel speaks of her longing to become pregnant with a child who would be "wanted and loved."

When I first became aware of the term "HIV positive" — personally aware — I was sitting in a hospital room with my partner. He had just been told, "You have the AIDS virus." No warning, no preparation. Then they turned to me, "Go down the corridor for your blood test, and then you must both come back next week."

My partner had been ill, in hospital for a few days, but everyone had avoided any talk of AIDS. When I asked if they had done an AIDS test, I was told not to be silly. Of course they'd done nothing of the sort. Then seven days later in another hospital room, my life was shattered in five minutes.

All the panic that went with the diagnosis flooded me every minute. I read the newspapers; I knew that he was going to die. Worse still, he believed it, and wanted to die as quickly as possible. This man had been ill, hospitalized with a stroke, and was not at his best as far as coping was concerned.

I spent the next few days trying to convince him that together we could face the problem and be stronger as a couple because of it. The strain was enormous, we would spend hours holding each other, with one or both of us, crying. I was desperate to talk to someone else who had already been in this situation.

On top of the immediate problem of supporting my partner, trying to convince him that it was worth the effort of getting well, was my own worry: what would the result of my test be? I went through long hours of soul searching. What if I was positive? "Condemned to die" was how I saw it at that point in my life. Or would it in fact be worse to be negative? What then? What could I do with my relationship? Could I continue? Would my partner reject me? I also knew that it would not be over if I was negative on this test. I would almost certainly have to go for another test in a few months time.

When we went back to the hospital it was with relief that we discovered that I was positive too. Then there followed once again a feeling of desperation: let's sell everything and go on a wild once-in-a-lifetime (or end-of-a-lifetime, as I thought) holiday. At this time, my partner was wonderful and I was the one struggling, near to tears all the time.

Perhaps the greatest blow was the end of our hopes to have a child. Wait a few years, see what happens was the advice of some doctors. On no account have a baby. It will kill you was the advice of others. How can you bring an orphan into the world? Why me? Why us? Were we such awful human beings, that we had to be punished like this? All around us the media was stressing the idea that only wicked people carry the AIDS virus.

The most horrible aspect of all this for me was not talking to anyone about it. My partner did not want to face up to things in the way that I did. It was just impossible to tell my sympathetic friend exactly how I was feeling. It was too fresh, too raw a feeling. Not really a feeling at all, but many rolled together. I went from desperation to determination that I would cope and fight every bit of the way to make my life, our life together, good for as long as it lasted.

It is now some time later. We have each developed our own way of handling the situation. I still need to talk to other people about my feelings in a way that he does not. He has gone through a period of totally rejecting the idea of the virus. But with more information about HIV and the gradual realization that there are thousands of others around in a similar situation, he will again talk about the problems of AIDS. I think the worst thing about the virus is the feeling of isolation and the fear that accompanies any step toward breaking the isolation.

I hope that people are now told of their status in a different way. But it is difficult to imagine, however you discover your positive status, that it would hurt any less. A few of the people that I have met as counsellors have been very well meaning, but have not offered me anything that I need. I just want to talk to someone who understands the hurt, the anger, without having to have everything explained. Other healthcare professionals have been wonderful and have respected my position.

I am still hoping to have a child. I know many of you will be horrified by this. I have been told that it is totally selfish, that I have no right to inflict the potential for suffering on an as yet unborn child. Who says I have no right? If I am lucky enough to become pregnant my child will be loved and wanted. Will that be further reason for rejection by society? I hope not.

I am still afraid of people finding out I am HIV positive, afraid of their reactions and prejudices. But I am no longer afraid of myself nor of my relationship with the man with whom I share my life. We have our ups and downs, depressions and moments of panic, but we are living full and rewarding lives both as individuals and as a couple. I want to ask you all to help end the ignorance and panic that go with the words "HIV positive." For many of us, they are a fact of our lives.

— JAE

ROSEANNE
CANADA

Roseanne was raised in Czechoslovakia and came to Canada as a teenager. She lives in Western Canada with her family.

Roseanne's piece is another exploration on the theme of HIV positive women having children. In contrast to Isabel who has only contemplated the possibility, Roseanne decided to have her two children after she discovered that she was HIV positive. Her bravery in choosing to have children in the midst of society's discouragement and discrimination is inspiring to other HIV positive women.

Some information about mother to fetus transmition of HIV needs to explained here. All babies born to HIV positive women carry maternal HIV antibodies. Within 18 months the maternal antibodies clear, and, according to the latest research, 70 to 87 percent of babies are then free of HIV.

It was a Tuesday morning I believe, in mid-February of 1987, when the call came. Ten days before this, I had found out that we were going to have our first child. We were both so happy at that time, so completely happy.

Then the nightmare began. "This is Dr. Smith's office calling," the voice on the other side said. "I have been asked to book you an appointment for this afternoon, Mrs. R. Could you please come in to the office about, let's say, 4:00 pm?"

I had no idea at that time how drastically that call would change my husband's and my lives. The happiness we had come to know just a short time ago was about to be shattered into a thousand little pieces.

I arrived promptly at 4:00 pm. In about twenty minutes, I was called into Dr. Smith's office.

"Hello, Mrs. R," he said. "How are you today?" After some preliminaries, he got right down to the reason I was called. "I hear from your family physician that you have just been handed a positive pregnancy test result," he said.

"Yes," I replied.

"I wish the news I have could be good news, but unfortunately it isn't."

"What is it?" I asked. "Is it the baby?"

"No," he said, "but I have some test results here that I should tell you about."

"But I haven't had any tests done in about ten months aside from my pregnancy test." I said.

"Not so. According to this, you have tested positive for the HIV antibody."

"What is that?" I asked.

"Have you ever heard of AIDS, Mrs. R? Have you ever heard of Rock Hudson?"

Then it was suddenly clear to me what this man was telling me. It was as if a sharp knife sliced through me right to the very core of my being. My life was being shattered in front of my eyes. I couldn't speak. The fear overwhelmed me. For me, for my unborn child, for my husband, for us. I wished he would just shut up. I wanted to scream but no sound came.

"I suggest that you contact your physician and discuss the details of an abortion. You will in all probability pass the infection on to your child and the baby will die."

How dare he suggest that I was going to kill my baby before it had a chance to live! How dare he tell me I was going to die! I was only twenty years old and someone had just handed me a death sentence.

I don't know how I made it home. I know I sat there and cried until there were no tears left, until I felt emotionally drained. And then my husband came home. How do you tell the man you love that someone has just sentenced you to death, and how do you explain that his unborn child may be born with AIDS? How do you explain that he himself could already be infected? There is no easy way.

But I did, and somehow I survived. The next three days passed in a haze of shock. I slept alone. He hardly slept at all. Locked away from each other, we both tried to contemplate what was happening to us. When we finally faced each other, we wouldn't touch. We just sat there and talked. We talked for about six hours and slowly through the anger and shock we decided,

> For better and for worse
> In sickness and in health
> Till death do us part

We had so much believed in those words, so young yet so

confident that nothing bad would ever touch us.

But that was then, and it all seems so long ago. My husband went for a test and it came back negative. Through the discrimination and fear and people urging us to abort our baby, we stuck together. But "for better or for worse" became mainly "for worse." But when the labour and delivery room was ready two months ahead of time because I was a "special precautions" case, we managed to love each other.

Then one beautiful Friday morning at 8:45 am our baby came into this world, screaming her will to live for all to hear. How proud we were and how scared for this little child, so tiny, so defenseless. We were so scared to love her, for we feared that if she should die, we would perish along with her. But she made us love her, more than life itself, for she was the continuance of life personified. She was life longing for itself and a new hope for us.

I was discharged two days later because the hospital was afraid the news of an HIV positive mom might spread around. I wasn't allowed to use the same bathroom as the other women and even had to use a completely different shower. My baby girl was with me all the time, as she was not allowed into the nursery and was an "infectious disease case" with "special precautions" labels all over. We loved her dearly and yet every time she would get a childhood disease or infection, we would fear that this might be the last time we would hold her.

In the beginning, she tested HIV positive, but we were told that those were just the maternal antibodies passed on to the child from the mother. And with each subsequent test they went down. When our little girl was barely two months old, I decided to defy the doctors and death and I became pregnant again. Call it risky, stupid, even downright dumb, I wanted another child. It was an act of defiance. It went against everything we were told. But we had faith.

This time the pregnancy was hard. I had a baby to care for and another on the way. I had numerous colds, pelvic infections. I bled early in my pregnancy and I was worn out to the point of total exhaustion more than once. Then we got the news of work in northern Ontario and decided to go where our prospects were good. Or so we thought. What a mistake!

In the beginning things were hard but beautiful. We lived in a small town. Clean air and lots of sun was always available. Everything was expensive and we didn't make much money, but we were happy.

At least until I became sick and my doctor ordered me hospitalized in the small town hospital. Then the parade of red stickers began again. One day I learned that while I was in hospital nobody would babysit for my husband or help him with our daughter. As a result he had to skip work, and since there were lots of contractors in the town, he lost the job. How I blamed myself those days and how I hated myself for putting him through this hell!

One day we took our little girl to the only doughnut shop in town and met up with a surprise. When we entered, the place fell silent and only whispers could be heard from behind our backs. Someone spit on the floor in front of us. At this point I was nearly in tears. They knew! There must have been a confidentiality leak at the hospital. We bought our daughter her doughnut and left. Thank God she was only nine months old.

The next day we found out more devastating news. I wasn't going to be able to have my baby naturally, or in town. I was to be scheduled to be induced at a hospital in the city five hours away. I was told when to go to the city and to report to Dr. X to be induced.

The next day, while my husband waited, the doctor broke

the amniotic sac of water. We spent the rest of the day wandering through the hospital. I had to carry my little girl on my hip, leaning on the wall to breathe through the contractions.

When the pain of my labour got so strong that I could hardly stand, we were faced with the problem of what to do with our little girl. It looked as if my husband and I were going to have to be apart while I had my baby. But then a small miracle happened. A woman approached my husband and told him that she had an HIV positive friend and that she was this person's nurse. She offered to babysit for us right there in the hospital. We were absolutely ecstatic. We wanted to be together when our child came into the world.

The delivery came two hours later and as our younger daughter entered this world we cried tears of joy. We were now complete. The four of us would face whatever life would bring and nothing would stop us. In the short moments after our child's birth, we decided that we were going to leave this city, the town we lived in, and take our family back home.

Our joy was premature though. The doctors miscalculated the dates and our daughter was born too early. She was a big girl at seven pounds, nine-and-a-half ounces, but there were other problems. Her bottom eyelids were turned inwards, eyes not quite ready for the outside world.

Ten days after her birth, she came down with a respiratory infection. She had to be hospitalized in the town hospital and there she suffered inhumane treatment. During the five days she was there, she was in a large metal crib, separate from the other babies. She was left to cry and at feeding time her bottle would be propped up on a blanket. How cruel to deny a ten-day-old baby human touch. The nurses only changed her when it was completely necessary. And then, they wore rubber gloves, masks, and gowns with hats. They tried to tell me that this was for my baby's protection. But if that was so, why was she plagued by a bleeding diaper rash from not being changed often enough? And why was her voice hoarse from crying? Her diaper rash cleared up when she got home, but her lungs and chest have always been sensitive and remain that way. She remained a shy and insecure child until the age of one, and to this day is afraid of strangers.

After we arranged an early release, we thought we could finally leave town. But life had other plans for us. I was so physically and emotionally exhausted by all the events and with caring for an eleven-month-old and a newborn, I came close to a nervous breakdown. I came down with severe migraines and was told that I couldn't be treated in the town hospital. I was sedated with Demerol, against my wishes, and flown to the city. There they performed a CAT scan to make sure that it was a migraine. Afterwards, still heavily sedated with Demerol, I was approached by another doctor. I remember talking with him about permanent sterilization and I know that in my state I wasn't hard to convince. The surgery was done the following day. It made me feel awful and I wondered how come they didn't want me to have babies so much. They caught me off guard and weak. I was plagued by a pelvic infection and severe bleeding after the surgery. I was also told to leave my room ten hours early and spent my time waiting for my husband in the hospital sitting room, while the staff scrubbed the room I had been in twice over, from top to bottom including the ceiling.

When the time came to leave northern Ontario, we had to sell just about everything we owned and worked so hard for. Everything went at a charity price. The town people didn't hide that they were happy to see us go. My microwave that my husband had bought me to make it easier to heat two babies' bottles had cost him 475 dollars of his hard earned money. It was still wrapped and 18 days old. They offered us a hundred dollars, and we had no choice but to accept. How much hurt I felt at this insensitive cruelty! My babies were the only bright things in our lives. We were literally run out of town. When we left, the only possessions we had were our vehicle, two baby cribs, some clothes and our dishes. We had our pillows, blankets and 980 dollars to our name to show for our move.

We have since closed a door on that chapter in our lives. Our love for each other is stronger than the hate we face. My husband remains HIV negative and our two beautiful daughters, aged two and three, are also negative. We just recently got the test results on our two-year-old with a big congratulations from our doctor. Our faith has paid off and our lives will continue in our children. We will teach them to love as we love and to respect life as we do. So maybe one day they will be able to say they were proud to be my children. I gave them life and in turn they brought hope into mine.

Back then, we lived in fear. Now we live with hope for a brighter tomorrow and we will never be sorry that we didn't listen to the doctors. For it was not their right to take a life that I had given. And I will never be sorry that I chose to do so.

LILLIAN HOPE
USA

Lillian is a public school teacher in Florida. She writes with great love about her relationship with Artie, from their first meeting through the seven years they spent together until his death from AIDS in 1990. Throughout many of these years, Lillian acted as his support and caregiver as he became increasingly ill. It is common that HIV positive women maintain these roles in their families, often at the expense of their own needs.

In this article, Lillian talks a lot about Artie's physical decline. She uses many AIDS related terms. For example, T4 cells (also called CD4 cells) are markers of the state of a person's immune system. A healthy person has a T4 cell count between 500 and 1,200. Lillian relates that Artie's first T4 cell count was 180 and that it rapidly dropped to 80 as he became increasingly ill. Artie's counts were low, but it is important to recognize that many people live long and well with considerably lower T4 counts.

What I remember most about the night we met were his eyes. He had the most beautiful eyes I had ever seen. They were many-coloured, and the night I met him they were a green-ish-gold. I saw him from across the street on a night in late April, 1983. It was a strange night; I remember the sky had an eerie orange hue. I was out walking, restless, in the Bronx. I remember thinking, "I'll go up this street, up one more block. Then it's too dark, too dangerous, to continue." In real-ity, to be out at all, alone, was dangerous. But that was the year my recklessness exceeded all reason, all bounds. I had long ceased consciously caring about my immediate circum-stances. I was driven by loneliness and the intense desire to find someone. And that night I found Artie.

As I walked up the last block, I looked across the street and saw someone who was lit up from the bright light of a bus shelter. The figure looked like he was glowing. I had to know who it was. It seemed as if he were watching me and, like a moth drawn to light out of the darkness, I hesitated, then crossed the street. I tried to be unobtrusive as I walked towards him, to pretend I was taking a bus too. A bus to where? I lived here. But he came to my rescue as I searched into those beautiful eyes, questioning me about the particular bus that would stop there. And I asked him if he was just out of the service. He had a suitcase with him and wore a camou-flage cap. He said, "No, I'm coming home from a trip to Florida." Then he proceeded to tell me about the town where I would spend seven years of my life and where I remain today. We talked for hours and spent the night together. And the summer. That was the beginning of my life with Artie.

We used to say that "it was a chance in a million" we met that way. I look back and try to sort out the whys of it all.

Why did I meet a man I loved more than anything, only to be left alone, childless, facing a fearsome disease, seven years later? But I wouldn't trade my time with him for anything in the world. He lit up my heart, and even though times were never easy there was so much richness in our love.

When Artie met me he saw a young woman who had so much going for her — I was a college graduate and had a good job — that he puzzled over why I had chosen to do dangerous things. The irony of it all is that I feel inside I would have died, physically and spiritually, had I not met him. I had hit bottom. I had drifted through one-night stands, going out alone in New York, hoping to meet someone who would care, never realizing the near-impossibility of accomplishing that with the path I had taken. Artie opened my eyes to this. As our relationship grew, the wall I had encased myself in began to break down and I began to care again.

Artie was up-front with me right from the beginning. On the bus, he said, "I've used drugs but I'm getting off them." That didn't phase me because I had once fallen in love with someone who also had used drugs in his past but had straightened out. I would have been much more alarmed if Artie had said he was an alcoholic. I simply believed what he said, that he was getting off the drugs. And that's exactly what he did. Because I lit up Artie's life just as he did mine. We spent about four months in the Bronx during which time he detoxed himself from methadone. He was irritable and difficult to deal with at that time.

One thing I remember so clearly, because it was a mystery to us, was that Artie had a problem with his skin. He had marks on his arms and legs and had burned himself in the sun trying to get rid of them. He used to say, "I thought I had AIDS." But that when he had gone to the doctors they had said, "Don't worry, you don't have that." Back then, in 1982, little was known about it, at least by whoever saw Artie. Other than that, Artie was gorgeous. He had black hair, dark eyes and a moustache. He was half-Italian and he looked it. And he had a wonderful sense of humour. He would tell his crazy stories over and over again, stories about places he'd been, encounters he'd had, and scrapes he'd gotten into.

Many of the stories he used to tell reflected his gradual realization, during seventeen years of drug abuse, of his need to change his lifestyle. For instance, he used to talk about his "Halloween car ride," an experience which was really a brush with death. He had gone to a wild party in upstate New York and was high. It was winter and the roads were slick. A friend asked him to drive to the store for more beer. They got into Artie's Fiat and took off. They were flying, doing eighty and ninety on roads Artie didn't know. His friend, who was also high, kicked back for the ride. Then his friend said, "Watch out for this turn, it's a mother!" But they were already in it – doing ninety on a hairpin turn leading down to a small bridge. Artie lost control, ran out of road, right before the bridge and they hit it broadside, flipping upside down into the water. When he felt liquid around his ears, Artie thought he was bleeding to death. Then he realized he was in this stream and he pulled himself through the car window. His friend was already on the bank, saying, "You've got to get the stuff out of there." They both knew they'd be arrested if caught with drugs in the car, so Artie dove down and got them. An elderly couple who'd heard the crash from miles away came to help and insisted he sit in their car. In the back seat, in a panic, for the police had arrived, he dumped a whole bag of pot out. The pot stuck to his wet pant legs. When he got to the hospital, the nurse asked him if they could cut the pants to get them off. Artie said "sure" and was relieved when the pot-laden pants were thrown away.

The part of this story which he repeated the most though, was when the state trooper took him back to the accident scene during the day. He showed him the skid marks which continued all the way down the hill for hundreds of feet. The trooper said, "God was sitting on your shoulder. You should be dead." And Artie knew it was the truth.

Our lives were happy during the first few years after we met. We didn't marry right away, but as our good friend Woodrow put it, we were "married by the heart." I became a teacher. Artie began working on construction. We enjoyed living in the country. Then we moved back to New York because I missed my family and my aunt was ill with cancer. I was miserable there; I missed Florida. In less than a year, we decided to return to the south. Only then the bad things started happening.

First, Artie hurt his back on a construction job. And he began having night sweats. He'd leave the sheets soaking wet in the morning. I had no idea what was wrong. Artie was afraid. I think, deep down inside, he suspected he had AIDS. He had always said after he kicked drugs, "I'm still not one hundred per cent." And he always said something that would frighten me. He'd say, "I don't believe I'm going to live past my father's age when he died" which was 46. He was right. I think he had a premonition.

I kept bugging him to take the HIV antibody test. I wanted to have a baby. How I wish now I had had one before I knew! That might sound selfish, but the longing for a child of his almost broke my heart after the diagnosis. By the time we found out it was too late, because he was having sexual problems.

I'll never forget the day we found out he was HIV positive. That morning, the morning we were to find out the test results, I felt like I was going to a funeral. Both of us had knots in our stomachs. We stopped to get coffee, then went to the place. Artie did not want me to come in. Looking back now, I wish I had. He went in. I prayed and prayed, out loud, "Please let it be negative!" When he finally came out of the building I watched him intently, hoping he'd give me a smile or a signal, anything to let me know it was okay. He never did. He walked as if a tremendous weight had descended on his shoulders. When he told me I just screamed, over and over, "No, no, oh my God – no!" He cried too, saying, "I just hope I didn't give this to you." He said all he wanted to do was to crawl into bed and hold me.

We stayed in a shocked numbness for months. I cried every day. I went through the motions of living at work. And I told three friends I worked with. Artie didn't want me to tell my family, which was a mistake. My sisters, ironically, both worked in the field of AIDS. They could have helped us. But the shock was too new and Artie fell into a deep depression. I began to gather information about the disease. We did go to a local hospital, but they told us they didn't use the anti-viral AZT. This was another terrible mistake. Our friend Woodrow told us to go to a bigger hospital an hour away. I'll never figure out why we didn't; they say hindsight is twenty-twenty. We found out much later that the large hospital had opened an AIDS clinic at the time we were looking for help. I still feel a tremendous sense of guilt about all this. I tried so hard, but it was never enough.

Since Artie was not yet on my health insurance policy, no local doctors would accept him. You see, we married a week after the diagnosis. I waited a long time to try to put him on my insurance because I had told everyone we were married long before, out of embarrassment. Finally, almost a year later, Artie got very sick. I got him on my insurance and took him down to a hospital in Miami. The Miami people did his first

T-cell count. At that time he was at 180. In a period of two months, he dropped to 80. He was running high fevers by August and I finally got him into a hospital. He stayed in the hospital for ten days, during which time I slept in a cot by his bed. He came home for a week, then went in for another five days, still running fevers. I was tested also, and found to be HIV positive.

My life had changed so much after his initial diagnosis. Suddenly, the future seemed black and uncertain. It had really taken us both a full year to begin to accept and deal with the disease.

After he began getting treatment, Artie improved dramatically for about four months. His improvement was due to AZT. Suddenly, I had hope again. He seemed like his old self again. After a few months, Artie began to have problems with his feet. He complained of burning sensations and would say his feet felt like "two bricks." I'll never forget the day he came home from the doctor and I looked at his face — he was utterly crushed. He told me, "The doctor said I would end up in a wheelchair." I felt an intense hatred of our doctor when he said that. My heart, again, felt broken in a million pieces.

I found out Artie had myelopathy (a disease of the spinal cord resulting in loss of muscle control). During this time I began searching for hope — hope in the form of new drugs. I called everywhere for information — Artie was now walking with a stick — and found nothing that could help with Artie's problem. But I refused to give up. Knowledge was my weapon, my strength. Within six months of the doctor's prediction, Artie had to accept a wheelchair. He fought against it as hard as he could. He had nearly drowned that summer, trying to stand in waist-deep water alongside his boat. I felt so sorry for him. It hurt me so much to see my proud man having to suffer so. And he took much of his anger out on me.

And too, I threw the disease in his face; resenting him for having used drugs in the first place and thus bringing this awful disease into our lives. Yet now I understand that were it not for his drug use, I probably would not have known him, nor he me, and I would never have missed knowing and loving Artie. But my anger and his made for some terrible fights and bitterness.

By November 1989, Artie's condition had grown worse. He could not walk, but still had his upper body strength. He had had a beautiful physique and was extremely powerful before he got sick. Now he used his arms to help himself from the couch to his wheelchair and from the chair to the tub. His loneliness broke my heart. Although I had to leave him every morning to go to work, I would call him each day during my lunch break.

We did not have a wheelchair ramp so in order to leave the house he would lower himself to the floor, slide out of the sliding glass door of our mobile home, and lower himself on to our riding lawn mower. Then he would ride around on his mower. He finally borrowed enough money from his relatives to buy hand controls for our van. Then he would drive the mower next to the van and transfer himself to it through the side door. The whole process was exhausting to him but he did not want to be trapped inside the house.

One day I asked Woodrow to put a step-up on the van to help Artie get in. Artie was watching from the front door of our mobile home. I was handing Woodrow tools. The next thing we knew, Artie had lowered himself down the stairs and was literally dragging himself towards us on his belly. He wanted so badly to help, to be of use. It broke my heart to see that and at the same time I felt a surge of pride for him. So many others might have pitied themselves and withered away. I just wish he'd had the strength to fight right after his diagnosis too.

Things got really rough for us in the last year. The doctor had been offering pain medication which Artie resisted at first, then accepted. He had a tremendous tolerance to drugs and, over a period of several months, lost control over the amounts he should have been taking and became re-addicted to painkillers. I am still angry at my doctor for prescribing so liberally to an ex-addict. Finally, I had to put him in a detox centre to help get things under control. Their answer was for him to go on methadone. When they told me this I was livid — I knew how Artie had tried to clean himself up — and I felt like this step was the beginning of the end. But he did go on the methadone program for pain management and I did realize he had a legitimate need for pain killers.

He was so angry at this time. And his anger towards me, when I was doing everything that I could, really hurt our relationship. It detracted from the kind of quality time I wanted to spend with him, the kind we used to spend. Finally a pastor from a nearby church came to see him. This visit changed Artie. He began talking with the pastor and accepted Jesus. Suddenly, his attitude completely changed and his anger dissipated. Now it was I who was angry, not Artie! But we did spend some important time together which was really precious to me.

We finally hired a nurse for Artie who later became a dear friend to me. Artie's nurse Sue filled the need Artie had to talk to someone else — someone who cared about him but was not personally involved in the situation. Someone, perhaps, he did not have to feel guilty about.

One weekend Artie was out driving, the next he was terribly sick. He said he was freezing. I knew he was in bad shape but I refused to believe that he would succumb to the disease. It was a sickening shock when he developed pneumonia. I thought, when I found out that he had pneumonia, that he would weather it and come home. It was not until I realized how critical his situation was — when our doctor kept shaking his head when I asked how Artie was responding to the antibiotics — that I utterly panicked. The wall I had built crumbled and I felt again the enormous pain I had blocked out for so long.

I stayed in the hospital with him when I knew how bad he was, just as I had years before. Only this time it was so much more awful. After three days in the hospital, they nearly overdosed him with morphine. I walked in and he was almost in a coma. They had to inject him with a drug to reverse the morphine's effects. After that, I didn't let him out of my sight. His condition steadily deteriorated.

I remember one night I crawled next to him on the bed and lay against his chest, with tears streaming down my face. He said, "What's wrong?" And I told him, "I guess it's that time of the month." Artie knew I got very emotional once a month, like clockwork. He smiled at me, but there were tears running down his cheeks also. We both knew why I was crying.

The next night he was gasping for breath. The hospital was doing nothing to help him. They told me they wouldn't put him on a respirator, that he said he didn't want one. I told them they were crazy, that they had to help, that it was his only chance to survive long enough for the antibiotics to work. I was nearly hysterical, pleading with three doctors while my husband lay gasping for breath. I begged my doctor and I begged Artie to tell them to put him on a respirator. Finally he asked our doctor, "What's in it for me?" And the doctor told him it was his only chance. And remarkably, Artie looked at our doctor, who was wearing a suit, and said, "Spiffy." Artie loved our doctor and trusted him.

They made me leave the room, but I could hear him gagging when they put the respirator down his throat. Artie had always told me he hated artificial life supports for people with no chance of getting better. He'd also said he would hate to die in a hospital. He wanted to die in the woods. Yet somehow I knew that if I put Artie on a respirator, he'd get off it alive.

That night was a nightmare. Sue and I tried to sleep in a hospital corridor. All night long we heard people running up the corridor to the intensive care unit. Sue knew, but I did not know till the next day, that they were running to revive Artie, who had ten cardiac arrests that night. I went to the ICU as often as I could manage and sang to him and talked to him and prayed for him. They kept him sedated. The next morning he woke up. I can't begin to tell you how I felt to see his eyes again!

The doctors told me I had a choice. I could attempt to take him home or he could remain there, but they told me there was no way he would survive. I already knew what I had to do. I had to take him home, to the place he loved. I couldn't let his life end in that horrible place. So that's what we did. We got him into an ambulance, attached to heart monitors and oxygen, and that whole ride home – because I insisted I be allowed to ride with him – I sang to him and talked to him. He kept trying to pull out the respirator. Before we made the decision, I asked Artie over and over, "Do you want to go home? Do you know what that means?" He kept saying yes, nodding his head.

When we got home, friends and our pastor were waiting. Artie got to see them and our cat. They took the respirator out. He spent some time alone with his pastor, and told him one of my favourite stories. And I held his hand and talked with him a little. The strange thing was that I began to have hope again. So did our nurse. And, I think, so did Artie. Just to have him home again made the hospital seem like a bad dream. But, after two hours, the heart medicine wore off. Mercifully, I was not in the room. Artie's physical therapist was feeding him a little soup when he went into cardiac arrest. Sue ran in there but they wouldn't let me. Artie looked at Sue, and said, "Help me, Sue." Then he died quietly in her arms.

Artie died on Memorial Day in 1990. It's been almost a year since he left me. I feel like there's an empty place in my heart. I miss him terribly. Sometimes when I'm at my chalkboard, teaching, the thought cuts through me like a knife, "Artie's gone." I feel like I will see him again when I die.

Some of the fight, the spirit, left me after he died. But then I get angry again, I want to beat this disease. I will beat it. I can't get Artie back, but I know he wouldn't want my fighting spirit to change. He would want me to go on living. And I will. I'd still like to have a baby.

I hope to get involved with the buyer's club that helped me obtain drugs for Artie. I'd like to work with children with AIDS. And I have faith that we will conquer this disease. If not, I have the man I loved more than anything waiting for me.

INGER M
DENMARK

In the series of poems which follow, written during the past three years, Inger speaks in great detail about her family and her love and her mourning for her husband. He was a hemophiliac who died of AIDS in 1987. Her identification with her husband's illness is reminiscent of Lillian, whose piece precedes hers on page 140.

The following poems were translated from Danish.

THE FLAME OF HOPE

It trampled into the security of our family life
transforming everything in a moment.
A chaos of emotions –
surprise, tension, fear and not least, hope.
Medical examinations.
A stay at the hospital.
It lasted a long time, I thought back then.
Three weeks of need, fear and hope.
Then a couple of years where it
Almost seemed as if nothing happened.
Then suddenly it returns.
The hospital and examinations.
Fear – could it be that?
Hope – no, no, it probably isn't.
Barely a couple of months later.
The results.
The shock – it was that.
Surprise – it can't be true.
Fear, but still hope.
The weeks pass.
A weekend visit at home.
Possible discharge next week.
Relief – it worked.
But no – in a flash, everything's changed again.
Crisis.
We wait – for what? Life or death.
Still – fear and hope.
Then one day
It worked – we made it.
Home again.
Oh – only for a short time.

Then again – the hospital –
home again – the hospital again – and finally,
home again.
Now we will have a sweet time.
Everything is just like before – I thought.
But – it is still here
and it is hard to face up to it.
About a month passes.
Fear and hope.
He grows more and more weak
and then – the hospital again.
The final stay we were later to learn.
It lasts a month.
I visit him every day.
The children come along a couple of times a week.
He sleeps a lot.
But in between he's awake.
We talk a little
then – he sleeps again.
And I wait.
For death, I thought.
No, hope was growing smaller
but I still hoped for life.
Then one day – that day.
I kept holding his hand
letting go of it reluctantly.
He was unconscious
but I called his name once in awhile
and told him I was with him.
Early in the evening
His breathing grows slower
and then – wasn't it about fifteen minutes later –
it stops completely.

I still held his hand
and broke into tears.
The small flame of hope was extinguished.

*

RETROSPECTIVE

Ten years of my life I lived with you.
In ten years we got used to one another.
To such an extent that now it's hard to comprehend
that you're no longer here.
We experienced ten years together.
We moved in together and got a dog.
You lost a friend shortly before we had our little boy.
We bought a house and fixed the garden.
We went on a camping trip.
I lost my father but you stood by my side.
We had our little girl.
In ten years we learned to know each other through good
times and bad.
You became ill and we grew even closer.
I always knew that I was fond of you
but death has shown me how much I have lost.
You weren't there
when our friends had their daughter.
The distance between life and death is so short.

*

A New Time

I hear your voice.
I see you before me.
There's something I want to tell you.
Where are you?
Your memory lives.
The old daily round
has become a new daily round.
But my thoughts sometimes make mistakes
and slip back into the old routines.
Last March I said good-bye to you
my companion in life.
You never returned.
In October, seven months later,
I said goodbye to you for the last time.
And yet, you have returned many times since.

*

Is That Supposed To Be A Comfort?

I want to be allowed to be bitter.
I want to be allowed to be angry.
I want to be allowed to feel sorry for myself.
Without always having to consider that there are those worse
off.
Is that supposed to be a comfort?

I have lost the one I love.
My own life is at risk.
My children may well lose both their parents.
All because of a treatment.

A deadly disease was injected into us.
So it must be legal to feel bitter.

If I have learned to live with my fate,
Learned to live with my fear,
Learned to live with my bitterness,
Then I suppose I should thank myself.
And not be thankful that there are others worse off.
How do you compare fates?
Perhaps they have learned to live with their troubles.

I feel sorry for the others.
I think it's terrible for them
and I understand that it's hard for them.
But why is it easier for me?
It remains unjust for us too.

It is no comfort that I could die of something else.
Because it is the fate
which has already hit me that I fear.
And that is the fear
I have to live with the rest of my life.

Just writing this I begin feeling guilty.
I'm not good at complaining.
I'm best at being happy.
And that's good.
But there's bitterness too.
Inside me.
Why can't I let it loose
With a good conscience?

*

MIDWAY

To live with HIV is damned hard.
You're not ill
and still you're not quite well.
Sometimes you think, "I'll be fine."
Is that because you suppress reality
and cling to hope?
At other times you face up to the fact
that all cases may develop into AIDS – mine too.
Does that mean that I've become a pessimist
who's given up hope?

You begin to notice every little change in your body.
Coughing, night sweats, swollen lymph nodes, fungi,
diarrhea.
Am I really aware of my body? Or am I just over-reacting?

Suddenly there are restrictions in your life.
You can't take a trip just anywhere you want.
Love is restricted.
And life will probably be restricted too.

Imagine, to be allowed to live just another ten years!
Imagine, to be able to see the children move away from home.
It would be like receiving a present.
And still it feels interminable.
Because for all those years I have to live with HIV.
Take my medicine day out and day in.
See the doctor month after month –
the rest of my life,
however long or short it turns out to be.

I am so unbelievably tired.
I sleep and I sleep and still I'm tired.
Is this because of a weakened immune system?
Is it a side effect from the medicine?
Or am I worn down by worrying?
I have to do so much by myself
and I don't have the strength
I'm so tired.
The least effort
and my body hurts and grows heavy and tired.
I feel unwell
I want to stay in bed and sleep, sleep.
– But I have to get up.
There is so much to do
and after all I'm not ill.

How will it end?
Illness? How? When?
And what about the children?
And the future? What is old age?
Time is so limited
and life has become so short.
Who will I share my thoughts with?
Who will comfort me?
Who will help me?
I feel so alone.
AIDS has taken my husband from me!

ROSA GUERRERO
MEXICO

The following interview between Rosa and her friend Ana is translated from Spanish. The situation that Rosa describes in this interview is common to many HIV positive women. She found out she was HIV positive after her husband became very ill. He died, leaving her to care not only for herself, but also for five children.

Rosa is struggling to survive. She has had to send her children to stay with relatives and she longs to be reunited with them. Yet in the midst of all these upheavals, she is still optimistic. She gets a lot of her support from the solidarity she feels with other HIV positive people. Through her AIDS support group, Rosa helps other HIV positive people, visits them when they are ill and tries to give them hope and encouragement.

Ana: Rosa, how did you find out you were HIV positive?

Rosa: I started to suspect when I found an envelope with my husband's positive results. But at that moment I didn't pay much attention to it, because it was more important for me to think about working to get money for my children. I thought he had gotten someone to fake the positive result, so I wouldn't make a scandal when I found out he had left me for another woman.

My husband used to donate blood. When the situation is urgent, they don't test the blood. They also pay donors for their blood. I never knew how much my husband earned. But he made comments that the buyers were thieves, and that for 500 millilitres, they only gave from 3,000 to 5,000 pesos.

Later I heard that a message had been broadcast on the radio that Mr. Guerrero should come to the Health Centre because he had AIDS and needed medical attention. Later, doctors, a nurse and the police went to the home of my husband's aunt and uncle and shouted from the street, "Does Mr. Guerrero live here?" His aunt came out and said, "No. He doesn't live here." They said, "We have come to see him because he escaped from the hospital and he has AIDS. He was under treatment and he needs to be under medical observation." They alarmed his aunt. And it wasn't true that he had escaped from the hospital.

Ana: Okay, that was about your husband. What about you?

Rosa: I became suspicious when he got sick in March 1989. He had diarrhea that didn't go away, and vomiting and weight loss. I really got frightened. Even though we didn't have relations with each other then, I thought that I could be infected because it hadn't been so long since we had. I took him to the hospital and they did a series of tests, but they never gave us the results.

The second time he got ill, I asked the doctor at the hospital if I could talk to him alone: " I want to ask you, what is AIDS?" "Why?" replied the doctor. "Because some time ago I found this paper which said AIDS virus positive, and it was in the name of my husband."

The doctor asked, "How long ago was this? How much time we would have saved if you had told me this from the beginning." The doctor told me that if one person is infected his/her partner has to be tested, and if there are children younger than five years old, they also have to be tested. The doctor said it was necessary that I get tested. He said that if I didn't feel any discomfort I shouldn't worry because perhaps I was not infected. That happens in many cases.

In May 1989, I went to see my doctor because of some pimples I had. I was almost certain that I was infected. When I came in, the doctor said, "I have two pieces of news, Mrs. Rosa, one good and one bad. Your children came out negative, but the bad news is that your test was positive."

I felt desperate, I felt that everything was finished. I couldn't hold the tears but, because there was a friend waiting for me outside, I pretended I was strong and I said good-bye to the doctor and went out. My friend asked what happened. "Everything is okay, thank you," I answered.

Ana: Did the doctor tell you where you could go for help?

Rosa: She told me about a group which would help with clothes for the children and medicine. Later I also went to the Mexican Foundation for the Struggle against AIDS.

Ana: When your family realized that you were infected, how did they treat you?

Rosa: One day at my uncle's house we had a discussion about my husband's death. My uncle said, "Rosa, is it true that Jose died of AIDS?" And I said, "Who told you uncle?" "Someone told me." I said, "I was told he died of 20 years of chronic alcoholism. I don't know of anything else." "If Jose had AIDS you wouldn't be here. You would have died already," he said.

Up to now they think that I am healthy, that I am not infected, and that my husband did not die of AIDS. The ones that did find out, because I had to tell them, were my mom, my dad and my sisters. I needed to know if they could help me with my five children, because this is my main concern. The oldest one is nine and the youngest ones are almost three. I took the twins to my mother for her to look after.

When I went to Oaxaca to tell my mother-in-law that my husband was sick, I brought my middle daughter and two of the other children. They stayed and later my mother-in-law sent me a letter saying that the children were not coming back and for me to send their papers so that they could go to school there.

Ana: How did your co-workers treat you?

Rosa: I worked as a street-seller, selling packages of books. I couldn't have a job with set hours because I had to look after my children. It was a program called "Program With Your Forehead High." My co-workers and I were strangers to each other. It was just "hi" and "bye"; there was no contact other than that.

Ana: They never realized about your husband?

Rosa: My husband was also selling. He went there once in a while and made some friendships, but they never knew. They asked me what he had, and I said typhoid, and that he hadn't sought medical attention soon enough, and there were complications. An older man said, "Yes, typhoid is very dangerous. I had it when I was very young and I got rid of it. But it was difficult." So no more comments were made and they believed it.

Ana: By now it is a little bit more than a year since you found out you are infected. How has your health been during this time?

Rosa: My health... good, good. The only thing is those allergic reactions I get because I take that medicine for the HIV. It is very toxic and I always have side effects. I have had problems from depression, but no other illness.

I know that to be HIV positive doesn't mean you die in 15 days or three months. With a good diet, good care and with some treatment, one can live better.

Ana: What are your main needs?

Rosa: I would say, what are not my needs? In the first place, I don't have my own house. My main preoccupation is my children. My need is for affection and to have my children by my side, because I have been living alone for more than a year.

Ana: You met various women who were HIV positive?

Rosa: Yes, when I was at the hospital, there was a woman who three years before had a blood transfusion when her baby was born, and she was there because she had toxoplasmosis. Another woman had also had a blood transfusion and that's how she got infected. She had come to the hospital with pneumonia and was being treated. I met various people who were infected through blood transfusions.

Ana: Do you feel that you can have sexual relations?

Rosa: Yes, one can have them, but there is always the risk. There is the fear that for one reason or another in a bad moment I may infect another person. The burden on one's conscience always exists. About needing... Of course, there are times when I need to have someone's company, not to be so alone, but it goes away.

Ana: What suggestions would you give regarding the care of women who are infected. What would you suggest to relatives or to the public in general?

Rosa: Well, to those who have relatives who are HIV positive, I'd suggest they inform themselves as much as possible about the illness. They should realize that with casual contact, just touching, they will not get infected. When they hear or know about an AIDS patient, they stare in amazement and they don't even want to get close. They feel that even with the air they're breathing they could get infected and that's not true. They need to know what the real ways of getting infected are. Then they should offer all the love and attention that is needed.

Ana: How have you managed with your children?

Rosa: I haven't told them. Not because I don't want to tell them, but because my parents prohibited me from talking to them about this. They live in a small town and the children could talk to others and my parents are worried about what people would say. That's why I haven't told them. My parents also say that I have this problem because I asked for it and that I have no right to involve other people, and my children the least of all.

Ana: You are doing organizing work with HIV positive people. Why do you believe it is important to work in groups?

Rosa: The women who are infected, the housewives, we are cloistered among four walls. We don't have any information, and we have the problem of having lots of children. We feel shut in. We don't know where to go, who to ask for help. I consider that it is very important to do organized work so that HIV positive women have a place to go to for help. Not to let them feel that because they are infected everything is finished and they should let themselves die. That was my case. I started selling and giving away my things because I thought I had only two or three months left. I realize now that I'm winning: one year and a bit already.

We visit people who are infected to invite them to participate in our group so they don't feel so lonely. We all have the same problem, and this way we spread the will to live. That's our main activity right now.

Ana: What things that you have organized have given you the most pleasure?

Rosa: The best thing is that the people show me their trust. When they talk to me about their problems, they are showing me that they trust me, that they really appreciate me, that it is not just for the benefit they obtain. They care about who they are talking to.

Ana: When you're with people who are in their terminal phase, what do you talk about?

Rosa: About simple things: their family, their children. I say "Why are you worrying? You'll get better." They say "I feel this, I feel that." I say "It will pass. It is a temporary discomfort." We want them to be relaxed. We don't know if they believe us or not, but at least they calm down a bit. We give them hope. I feel very good when I see I can diminish people's pain.

DAMBUDZO
ZIMBABWE

Dambudzo is a young black woman who integrates her traditional customs and beliefs with Christianity. What Dambudzo has to say about living with AIDS and how she says it relates to her own culture.

After dealing with the initial shock of her husband's infidelity, her diagnosis as HIV positive and the death of a child, Dambudzo has turned her life around. She became involved with the Mashambanzou AIDS Crisis Centre in Harare, Zimbabwe. This Centre provides counselling, peer support and housing. It is supported in part through fundraising activities such as the sewing workshop which Dambudzo has recently started.

HOW ILLNESS HAS AFFECTED ME AS A WOMAN AND A WIFE

I was sent for more examinations and blood tests. The doctors said we suspect that you have got HIV in your blood.

After that they sent somebody to explain everything about the disease. I was shocked. I found it hard to accept. At first life was bitter and sour, or it was just like a dream. I started to think very hard. Where did I get it from? When? From whom? How am I going to live among others? What is going to happen to me? Is it my husband? Let me say, this husband of mine wasn't satisfied with one woman. Yes, it was very easy for me to point at my husband. He was an unfaithful husband. Sometimes he left me at home and went for other women. I would even go and pay his girlfriend's accounts. He would go to the racetrack, the Mashonaland Turf Club, with so many different girlfriends at a time, leaving me at home.

I worried myself with so many questions and thinking too much, which led me into a depression which was not good because I thought about suicide. Thinking too much wasn't helping me, but making me feel worse.

Once you have got the virus, the best thing to do is to find comfort. Seek ideas from the counsellors and psychologists. Ask everything you would like to know about the disease. Because you have HIV, an STD, or AIDS does not mean the end of life.

Believe me, for I am telling you out of experience. I have got the virus and I am suffering from it as did my lastborn child. She passed away September 10, 1989 when she was two-years-and-two-months old. See how innocent people suffer because of one's guilt. Let me not talk about the death of my child because it hurts me very much. I know she really suffered. As her mother, I was always with her until the last minute.

In 1986, I got married to a caretaker. This caretaker of mine was working at the Church. I trusted him very much and thought I had made a good choice to marry a Christian. But to my surprise this husband of mine was quite different from what I thought. This man wasn't satisfied with one woman. He used to go to the Borrowdale Racetrack for betting. When I was six months pregnant, my problems started. I told my husband that it was time for me to go to the prenatal clinic. He said, "This month I don't have enough money. You will go next month." When another month was finished, he said the same thing as before.

In this time of discovery I also discovered that this husband of mine had worked for the church for 20 years, but had no savings account, no bed, not even wooden chairs. Nothing that showed this man had worked for so many years. Where was his money going? Girlfriends, the racetrack, and girlfriends' credits.

That's how my problem started. When we stayed together during my pregnancy, he was attacked by VD about six times, but he refused to go to the doctor. When I was seven months pregnant the Lord came to help me. God provided the reverend's wife who came to me and asked me if I was attending the prenatal clinic. I replied that we didn't have money. She said, "Tomorrow, I will take you there." Early in the morning, I got up and got ready. We went to the clinic where she parked the car and remained inside. She sent me to join the others who were standing by the door. The nurse in charge came and asked everybody for their pay slips. I went back to the reverend's wife and said I didn't have a pay slip for my husband. We went together to the nurse. Again she asked how much my husband earned a month. I said I didn't know.

Everybody stared at me with surprise. They thought maybe I was trying to be rude. The reverend's wife, without saying a word, took out twenty dollars and paid for me.

After everything was done, I was told that my blood was negative for syphillis. What a big surprise, since I was sleeping with my husband who had all those sores. If I had said no, he would have said, "Pack your things and go right now, at midnight. If you tell anybody that I am sick then don't come back. Stay away forever." Where would I go while I was seven months pregnant?

Indeed, I was in real trouble for sure. I tried to tell the nurse. I explained how he was sick. The nurse said, "Tell him to come here." I told him but he said, "No. I will not go. I will rather go to the *n'anga* (traditional healer), than the doctor." I went and told the nurse again. Then she said, "Now we can't help you because your blood was negative. If it was positive for syphilis, we could force your husband to get treated."

My baby was due June 1, 1987, as the doctor and nurse said. To my surprise June 1 passed without my beginning labour. At first there were no problems, but when the second week passed, the problems started. I was now feeling tired each day. Suddenly on June 11 I went into labour. I was a mother of two already, but the pain of this third pregnancy was quite different from the others. I delivered the baby at 2:00 am, after 12 hours of suffering. By the time I delivered, I was breathing by means of oxygen. The baby was 3,320 grams. A healthy baby everybody said, but nobody knew that the HIV had been passed from father to mother to this otherwise healthy baby.

We came to know this when I was seriously sick after the birth of the baby. I stayed at home for only seven days. On the eighth day, I was admitted to Parirenyatwa Hospital. I had abdominal pain, diarrhea, vomiting, chest pain, swelling and tenderness in every part of my body, and I felt very weak. The abdominal pain was coming in intervals, just as though I was going to deliver another baby. Maybe there was another baby about to come out. I even mentioned it to the doctor and said the pain was just the same as labour pain. This is the most terrible disease I have ever had in my life time.

After so many examinations and blood tests, I was told on July 7, 1987 that I was carrying the HIV in my blood. I was shocked, because I didn't understand it as I do now. I thought that it was the end of my life. I even gave all that belonged to me with my relatives. And so many people are still saying there is no AIDS. They are fooling themselves for sure.

*

Here are some helpful hints on how to live with HIV:

1. Become a believer. Go to church every Sunday. This will help you to find comfort in the word of God. To find comfort from somebody who understands the Bible better than you is a good idea.

2. Follow everything that is said by your doctor, psychologist and counsellors, and follow your check up dates correctly. Be careful about the people you take advice from, because this disease is a new thing in Zimbabwe. Some people will frighten you. Take it easy and forgive them because they don't understand it.

3. Keep yourself busy all the time, but not by working too hard. Read books that can help you to forget about the heavy burden you are carrying. Listen to music such as church

songs. These will comfort you. Sewing clothes and cross-stitch can make you busy also.

4. Ignore all the world systems of pleasure, for example going to films, bands, beerhalls, etc. Don't be a street walker. These will lead you to the temptations of wanting to enjoy the world system. The result of enjoying yourself will be the spread of the HIV virus to other innocent people. Ignoring the world systems and all the sexual practices will also make the virus sleep for a while. I have experienced this.

Let me tell you, my brother or sister, aunt, uncle and everybody who knows that they have HIV. God will punish you for spreading it purposely. It's just the same as taking an axe to chop off someone's head. If you know that you have the HIV in you, and you spread it on purpose, then you are a murderer. Be merciful to the other innocent people.

5. Identify the people to whom you can tell your problems. They must be the people you trust, who understand about this new disease. Don't tell everybody. If you do so, some people will run away from you because they don't understand how the disease gets from one person to another.

6. There is another secret in this virus. The virus's actions are just like a tortoise moving in the bush. If it hears a noise or footstep, it stops moving and listens. Then, as the noise comes near, it will hide its head and legs inside the shell. That is the same with the virus. If you avoid or stop sexual practice everyday, the virus will sleep for a while. It's only by turning away from the world systems that you will survive for a while.

Is AIDS in Zimbabwe? Not in the country only, but in human

beings like me. Brothers, sisters, uncles, aunts, grandfathers and grandmothers, beware of AIDS. Now I am telling you. Believe that there is this disease that they call STD, HIV, AIDS. Believe it now and take the steps to avoid getting it or to stop spreading it.

JANE SHEPHERD
UNITED KINGDOM

Born and raised in England, Jane continues to work part of the year in Zimbabwe as a freelance illustrator. When she is in London, she tries to promote links between the AIDS campaigning forces in England and those in Africa, and to instill an interest and awareness about Africa.

The frontispiece which opens Positive Women *was created by Jane for the Mashambanzou AIDS Crisis Centre in Harare, Zimbabwe. Three of her other illustrations follow. The first illustration, entitled "Girls have the right to say no to sex," was produced for the Zimbabwean Ministry of Health's AIDS Control Program. The message is aimed at young girls who need support and encouragement to defend themselves against unwanted sexual advances. Traditionally, men in Zimbabwe look for partners younger than themselves and, now particularly, for virgins in order to avoid infection. The next illustration is a graphic celebrating World AIDS Day 1990 which she designed for the Women and AIDS Support Network in Harare. The last illustration, entitled "Let there be no more fear and ignorance," is a T-shirt design which Jane has produced and sold at AIDS fundraisers.*

— Jane Shepherd

WORLD AIDS DAY 1990

— Jane Shepherd

LET THERE BE NO MORE FEAR AND IGNORANCE · JOIN TOGETHER TO FIGHT AIDS ·

—Jane Shepherd

177

IMANI HARRINGTON

USA

Imani has three pieces of work in Positive Women. *Her short poem* A NEED TO BE *opens the anthology. Imani wrote the following essay after she visited one of the AIDS sanitoriums in Cuba. She addresses a very controversial topic: the quarantine of HIV positive people. The threat of quarantine creates a climate of fear amongst HIV positive people and is one reason that many people are secretive about being HIV positive.*

In Cuba, people who are diagnosed with HIV must live in AIDS sanitoriums, apart from the rest of society. Cuba's measures are extreme, but quarantine has been suggested as a method of stopping the transmission of HIV in almost all other countries. In this essay, Imani defends the Cuban system and points out that although quarantine is not an official public health policy in the United States, it exists unofficially in many ways.

Her poem "AID of America" is a powerful performance piece which explores some of the themes of her essay. It links AIDS to the history of Black women's oppression in the United States.

California based, Imani is a dancer, performer and activist.

AMERICAN QUARANTINE: ISOLATION, ALIENATION, DEPRIVATION

It is difficult to raise issues about Cuba, as I am often mistaken for a Cuban apologist. Unfortunately, many people still blame Cuba for its past mistakes. After travelling to Cuba on an educational trip to visit the controversial AIDS Sanitorium, as a lesbian living with HIV, I discovered the propaganda that has been levied against the Cuban government was unfounded.

The AIDS Sanitorium in Santa Diego is not a "concentration camp" as so many call it. Neither the gay population nor heterosexuals infected with HIV are left to die. Instead those who are HIV infected in Cuba and their families are supported psychologically and financially. Their families receive counseling and those who cannot work are paid their full salary. Family members are allowed to visit and stay overnight. Those living at the sanitorium can visit home and are now being intergrated back into their communities to resume the jobs they once held.

What many in America have defined as "quarantine" reminds me of what has been defined as democracy. "Democracy" in America is the existence of the homeless, welfare lines and the uninsured. The American concept of quarantine can be seen in prisons such as Vacaville where the AIDS and HIV positive population is isolated. In Cuba, absolute patient care, the value of life and human welfare are a part of being "quarantined." I do not profess that the Cuban quarantine is the most moral or effective way to accomplish the goal of stopping the spread of the virus. But frankly, I would rather be "quarantined" in Cuba than in America.

The support given to those living at the sanitorium is so much better than the medical and psychosocial support that I can't even begin to access in America. Anytime I am forced to pay an outrageous premium of 279 dollars per month for insurance which guarantees that I will receive medical attention, I feel quarantined. When I cannot receive disability because this disease is not defined in women as it is in men, I feel quarantined. When someone can be treated with quality care and I cannot, I feel quarantined. When I am told that in order to receive health insurance I must be employed, I feel quarantined.

I have been negated, restrained and repressed as being someone deviant. I have been emotionally strung out and held hostage by the outer laws that have so forcefully governed my existence as a black woman in America. Here in America I am the "alien," the "foreigner" with the AIDS virus. My people have been set apart, divided and damn near conquered in this society. We have been locked away in ships, in jail cells, in cold coffins. We have been ostracized and criticized. Our culture, tradition and languages have never been accepted. If this is not American quarantine, then tell me what is?

America and Iraq are the only two countries in this world that do not allow people with HIV or AIDS to enter their country. America and South Africa are the only two countries that do not have a national health plan. In Cuba, where people come first, health care, education and social security are free to all. HIV positive people there are not burdened with fear because they know that their medical needs will be attended to. They do not have to worry about whether the doctor or dentist will fear their HIV status or if their insurance will be discontinued. They do not have to worry about paying insurance premiums or about how they would pay for AZT if they requested it. If this is a form of quarantine, then I prefer it to "democracy."

AID OF AMERICA

Small bones crushed by
        the foot of racism
will be placed in an
        archaeologist's grave
precious red wet eyes run
        deep charged
with blood dripping
        staining our bodies
onto canvases to be hung
        in a dying gallery
blending colors of pain-o-
        sorrow-o-grief
into the heart open lonely
        space of a mother's
        mouth
crying for the loss of her
        child
the rich sweet acrid taste
        of a mother's love
has been lost in this war/

I am, we are, they are,
        you are not IT a veteran
in AMERICA
with the aids of
        AMERICA
crossings life's war
combatting a disease
        infiltrated
with the aid of
        AMERICA

by society's lack of
     responsibilities
myths told, legends, will
     die when a hungry
     child cries
with the aids of
     AMERICA
those spared will cry too
     because
their mothers have died
     from a disease
with the aid of
     AMERICA
when a child will crawl to
     search for her mother's
heated chocolate breast
     to suck for the milk of
     love juice
run wild and out
with the aids of
     AMERICA/
To make your living at
     night under the red
     light
girl you will be charged
with the aids of
     AMERICA
hissing chimes the men
     throw dimes to slide
on your wet body your
     blood line is a crime
for she is a child of the
     tenderloin/

To be raped before and
        receive a disease
To cry out under the
        black night
as an act of your pain will
        be relegated
shame on your name
        when they hear
you got the aids of
        AMERICA/

To be disregarded disassociated
        to lay in a bed
for a father to spit upon a
        beautiful face and
race to the mirror cause
        you are a black woman
        in America
A lesbian's choice you are
        not to have a face or
        voice-stop
denying lesbians do die
with the aids of
        AMERICA/

How can we forget what
        it means to lay down
on a pissy homeless bed
        with cardboard
        hanging
over cold black heads
        lynching fear
        Lest we be reminded of

the blood that dripped
off southern black trees
became a disease
whenever her cycling
blood the one mad
method
racism in aids invades our
people's minds
destroys the life lines lest
we be reminded that
BEIN' a black woman in
this country is to look
at the racist virus has us,
got you and me
to look in the lookin
mirror
you will be reminded that
BEIN' a black women
you will be attacked
by the racist regime like
Hitler's theme
turns to a thesis of
disease released to our
families

The crumbs of racism will
fall off into
your child's poor wet
eyes and bleed
with the aid of
AMERICA/
little children will suffer
from a never

to be gotten disease with the aids of AMERICA
How can it be forgotten
      when we are treated
as scapegoat vessels for
      the blood of the virus
moving through us
      without consent
to be forced not to abort
      the choking life
of our babies breath
      which ultimately
leads to our deaths
with the aid of
      AMERICA
with the aids of
      AMERICA/
To pass on this legacy as
      a black crime
Again the old red white
      and blue stands true
for who's got who
with the aids of
      AMERICA
Reagan, Bush and Quayle
      will not hail
for the causes of this
      disease but when
San Fransisco shook 7.3
      they respond
      immediately
– as the marina seems
      greener when they
      bury black tinas who

lost their lives
with the aids of
    AMERICA
with the aids of
    AMERICA

YAN SAN OYA
U.S.A.

Yan San Oya was born and raised in a traditional Puerto Rican family. In dealing with her HIV status, Yan San has drawn on many different spiritual sources. She thanks her family for the spiritual values which they passed on to her and which have given her the strength to deal with her life. Her family is Catholic, but also practices Santeria (a voodoo folk religion found throughout Latin America).

Currently living in California, Yan San works with many feminist and Latina groups and AIDS projects. The following is an excerpt from an interview with Yan San which was part of a promotional video for the Center for AIDS Services in Oakland, California, an AIDS service organization with a spiritual focus.

It has been a year since I have been diagnosed with ARC. I have a God within that protects me and takes care of me. He has done so in the past year.

I was raised with different aspects of different religions. Though, I was raised a Catholic, my parents also practised spiritualism. People in my culture, they practise Santeria, which is believing in saints like Chango and Oshun. My parents are very spiritual and I thank them for passing it on to me. If something happens I pray to God to help me or I pray to Santa Barbara to protect me. And I always feel that my mother sends all these forces to help me.

Growing up and becoming an adult, I joined other religions. I practised Buddhism. I also worked with a Quaker organization and learned their way of relating to the God within. I believe that there is love and that love flows through me. And I can share these beliefs with many different communities, people from many different backgrounds.

I am also recovering from a drug and alcohol addiction. Being in a program of recovery, I got in touch with that higher power and it just reinforced the beliefs with which I was brought up. The mind can heal the body and if there is peace within, if there is some serenity, then the body will respond. I believe that I have a higher power that takes care of me. I just have to nurture that power.

It is not easy at times. There are days that I don't have any hope, when I am totally overwhelmed. When that happens, I need to get in touch with myself and sit back and reflect. I just need to get in touch within and maintain and nurture that part of me, the spiritual aspect. It is always there.

Being in contact with other people gets me out of myself. It is like a medicine. Giving out love and getting it back in exchange heals. Working with other people and volunteers and helping others has helped me love myself and understand and heal myself.

I have had the sense that people don't want to get near me because I have a virus that can kill someone if we exchange our body fluids or we have intimate contact. Getting a massage and just feeling in touch with someone is like embracing. It is important to touch and have that communication. It is wonderful to share with someone who is not afraid to touch me. At the same time this physical communication is silent. I think that is important, because the communication is deeper, more intense that way.

LEETIA GEETAH
CANADA

Leetia is an Inuit woman from Baffin Island in the Northwest Territories. Leetia's first language is Inuktitut. Her submission is a transcription of a talk which she gave at a forum on Aboriginal Women and AIDS organized by the Two Spirited People of the First Nations in Toronto. At the time that Leetia gave this speech, she had spoken publicly only once before. She spoke very movingly without having a prepared speech.

My name is Leetia Geetah. I am originally from Baffin Island. I was raised in a very good family. My stepparents took care of me while I was growing up and I lived with my family until I was 21, the year my stepfather died. But I put myself in a situation I said I would never get into. I said I would never drink or smoke. But I learnt I will never say "never," because when I said I'll never touch anything, I lied.

I quit school at 17 to take care of my stepparents, because they both had cancer at the same time. I stayed home during most of my teen years which made me proud of myself because I took care of them. I paid them back for what they did for me. I fed them and cleaned them. There was also no one else in my family that wanted to do that.

I was so close to my stepparents. When they died, I felt so alone even though I had six sisters and seven brothers. So I would not feel so alone, I started drinking at 21. I enjoyed it and it helped me get my feelings out, which I thought was great.

I drank quite heavily and I started screwing around. I realize now I drank and smoked so that I wouldn't feel any pain and would be in a good mood around people who I didn't want to turn down. I was also a sexaholic. I loved sex.

A few years ago, I went into a coma for one month and a half. I know what caused the coma: meningitis. That same year in the month of August, I found out I was HIV positive. I can't tell you how and where I caught it. It was probably when I was drunk. I didn't know HIV was around my hometown. There were commercials on TV about it. I thought, "It's not up here. It' s not in our home community."

When I found out I was HIV positive, the only thing that went through my head was: "Why me, Lord? Why are You putting me in this situation? Two months ago I was in a coma. Now I find out I am HIV positive." I blamed God for it. I blamed Him for everything. Why did You take my parents? Why did You put me in this situation?

I did not tell my family. I did not talk about it. I kept it inside me and I drank even more in order to avoid thinking about it. I became an alcoholic. Everytime I was sober, it was in my head and I was beating myself inside. When I am in a tub, I scrub myself because I don' t feel clean. I ended up in a hospital from scrubbing myself too much. Being HIV positive has made me feel I'll never be clean anymore.

I felt I was the only native Inuit Canadian who had HIV. I moved from my hometown which I did not want to move from. I had lived there for the first 21 years of my life. I had three choices: Ottawa, Montreal or Yellowknife. I decided to move because I just couldn't face up to staying up there, where I am from. I chose Ottawa because I have cousins there. I thought that they would be supportive. I thought wrong.

My cousin has come to me when she has pains in her joints, asking me if I had pains like that before I found out. I am the only person that she turns to for an answer. She has a fear of sitting with me, but she has the guts to ask me all these questions. She bothers me when she comes asking me all these questions about pain. I told her: "I am not an expert. Why don't you go to a doctor to find out if you are a carrier? I cannot answer any of your questions at all." She tells me she cannot face that.

My cousin has jeopardized my life. I was making good friends in Ottawa. She was telling them that if you sit in a room for so long with me, you can catch it. So she scared my friends away from me and it really hurts, especially being called a human germ. One time when I got so angry at her, I told her, "I am going to be so glad once you have become one." I later went up to her and said, "I am very sorry for what I said. Please don't take it too serious."

I have often wanted to die, but I have a son. It's going to be hard for me to tell him I am a carrier. He is three years old. He doesn't understand yet. It got to the point where I couldn't talk with anybody, so I talked with him as though he understood. I told him I was angry at myself, that I wished I had the power to get this disease out. Everytime I cried in front of him, when I was alone with him, he patted my back and said "mom" as if he understood every word I had said. I would have killed myself if it weren't for my son, because I know he needs a mother.

At the time I found out I was HIV positive, I was breast-feeding my son. When I was breastfeeding him, I thought I probably would pass it on to my little boy, who is innocent. I had my boy tested and I am very happy he is negative.

It was really hard for me to start going out to make a speech. It really is hard to talk about it. At times it makes me think "What am I going to say?" I might say something wrong. But I told myself I must start giving out messages to native people, who are my people, to be careful. People have to learn about this. That is why I agreed to speak in public. I want to tell my people: "Quit the drugs before you get worse. I know, I am in it."

I am working on learning more about HIV and AIDS before I start going to settlements to speak. I am doing my best to be strong and when I don't have to think about it, I don't. Because everytime I start thinking about it I want to go out drinking so I won't feel pain. But I know alcohol is not going to help me get rid of it. It is going to put me in the hospital forever.

I went to Vancouver in January and since then my courage has grown to return to my community and speak in public in my language about HIV. People up there don't know what HIV is. They think only gay and lesbian white people get it.

Since I spoke at the conference in Vancouver, I am more relaxed. I am so grateful that there is a lot of support for me. I need a lot of support so I will be able to talk about how I feel to the point where I won't have to keep anything to myself.

I am grateful that they are not calling me a germ like my kind of people do. I have brothers and sisters. Most of them reject me. I hope they will get to a point where they can accept me again. They were so close to me when our stepparents were alive.

I couldn't accept being a carrier of HIV for a long time, but now I do. I accept it cause I'm stuck with it. I really hurt myself and I hated myself before I started accepting it. I am more happy now. I must live with it. I realize there is no one to blame, only myself. Now I am willing to accept what I am and I am happy that I am alive today, so I am able to go to communities and settlements and speak and give out messages.

Now I am coping and doing my best. At times I just wish that I could die in my sleep. But when I wake up in the morning, I am grateful to God that he takes care of me. I take it one day at a time. I just couldn't throw it away. I am praying to my God to support me and lead me so I can help my people to understand more. I am grateful now. I feel a lot better today.

I'll be there for people who cannot accept what they have. I'll be there to teach them that they have supporters everywhere.

MIRINDA LAFAYE

CANADA

Mirinda LaFaye speaks about her name and her poetry: "My name is Mirinda LaFaye. It is a name I've taken, so I can say the things I need to say without fear. It is an ancient name taken from the Fairy People of the Celtic Isles and Normandy. Mirinda is a women's name for warrior, LaFaye is French for fate. Warrior and Fate: this just about sums up what I've been presented with since being diagnosed HIV positive."

"This first poem is how I felt when I was diagnosed HIV positive in May 1987. It isn't how I feel now, but reflects my pain, loss and isolation at that time which I wish to communicate to others. It's about being inappropriately cut off from my birth rights and my whole and integrated connection with nature."

No Thine Sweet Kingdom Come

Under tall trees on fragrant dry whispers
    There lie dream seeds sprouting.
Promises wither in the noon day sun.
    Ravens on the wing circle tall trees
On lofty hot updrafts.
    Hear their mocking laughter move from sky to wave,
    To twinkling eye and knowing glance.
    New promises are made at the dawning of a day;
Just a day and I walk the rocky shore.
Will I cross over soon?
    Dry whispers cry to the dream seeds:
    Beware!
    Promises wither in the noon day sun.
Many are the bleached dry bones of youth now passing,
I wear them on my hip
I hang on promises withering and the hope of dream seeds
    sprouting.
I can do nothing but, I am dry bones.
I am promises withering in the sun.
    My dream seeds are not my own, they were stolen,
    Gone away, stolen.
No justice will be done, No thine sweet kingdom come.
Now Holy, Holy, Holy, now not and never more to be
    Sweet, See?
Into retirement I step, the cord of replication cut,
First cry of life refused.
They were stolen, gone away, stolen. I teeter, pause, and
Then proceed. I shake the tears from out of my eyes.
    I enter down the long dark hall
    Shadows from the valley of death have been imported.
    And Yeah...I shall walk.

– Mirinda LaFaye

197

Her song and dance do comfort me. My weary way I'll wander
Till no more my sun shall rise and never more
My morning star to set on the haze of lazy days.
  Under tall trees dreaming
  I lie on fragrant whispers
  Of ancient secrets dreaming.

BLACK CEMENT DEATH GETS SERIOUS AND LIGHTNING
STRIKES TO MAKE THE GROUND ELECTRIC: SOME
GRASS GROWS

Warrior, are you wandering lost?
Where are you parked tonight?
        Are you breathing the poisoned lies
Of Black Alley Death deep into your lungs?
        Are you walking the solid yellow
Line? And just where are your little sisters?
Who knows your battle?
            Invincible Bear, who sees you?
        Warrior, go lie on the grass.
        She has a message for you:
BLACK CEMENT DEATH GETS SERIOUS AND
STARS START FALLING DOWN FROM HEAVEN.
LIGHTNING STRIKES AND MAKES THE GROUND
ELECTRIC – SO FLOW THROUGH THE RIVERS
OF LIGHT TO WHERE YOUR LOVE IS NEEDED.
THERE IS NO TIME TO WONDER WHY.

— Mirinda LaFaye

NICOLE FOLLONIER
SWITZERLAND

Nicole has experienced many hardships, yet has always managed to overcome them. Left on her own from an early age, her father dead and her mother often absent, Nicole had trouble coping and turned to drugs and alcohol. After several years of failed jobs and failed relationships, she was hospitalized for hepatitis and at the same time found out that she is HIV positive. Her boyfriend had knowingly infected her.

And yet Nicole speaks with excitement about the life that she has created for herself since this time. She is now sober, has supportive friends, and has learnt how to nurture herself.

Nicole is very active both within the AIDS community in Bern and is a speaker in schools. Nicole is also the artist of the drawing on page 269 of this book.

I was born in June 1966 in Zurich. My parents lived there, but always separately. Since my mother worked and travelled a great deal, I stayed with many different families. With them I always had to act the well-behaved, dear, helpful Nicole, always obeying.

School was always bad. I was always amongst the worst students and was laughed at and teased. In my spare time I sat for hours at a time in front of the TV, alone. When I was 13 years old, my father died. I had only seen him rarely. He was an alcoholic and it was written all over him. I loved him very much. I began to hang out and turned to alcohol and drugs. At school I was sent out of class to see psychologists.

After I finished school, I thought: get away from Zurich and my mother whom I hated, hardly ever saw and then only to fight with. So I began my one year apprenticeship in agriculture. Soon I ran away again. I was treated like a kid from the big city and I was in turmoil 24 hours a day. I could not set boundaries for myself.

Then I lived with a family of five for one year and by the end of it I had become the hard working cleaner, cook and nurse. But where was my self?

After this I worked in a home for handicapped children. But very soon there again I was in turmoil. Alcohol and drugs helped me to switch off now and then. My first boyfriend whom I had known for six months suddenly wanted more from me: sex. I had not been educated about sex, did not know my body and was used to giving whatever was asked of me. But after about six months, I could not stand what I considered to be rape. Then followed a time when I over ate, until I expanded like a balloon and couldn't cope. Then the opposite happened and I stopped eating. I finally fainted and woke up in hospital.

Pressure was put on me to get an education. So in April

1986, I began training as a governess for handicapped children. I liked the work, but I simply could not create boundaries. I had one day off a week. On this day I spent time with my new boyfriend Hampi. I did everything so that he would not go back on hard drugs. My feelings and needs were constantly bungled and drowned with alcohol and drugs.

In the summer of 1987, I could not stand it anymore and one day I left. I went with Hampi to Italy, Greece, Turkey and India. I was always searching for something which I probably should have searched for within myself. This journey taught me a great deal. But it was also hard and ugly. I got raped and Hampi returned to drugs. In India, I became very sick and with my last strength I returned to Switzerland. There I was hospitalized with hepatitis. One morning the doctor came and told me I was HIV positive.

I had no knowledge that a test had been done and the results were thrown at me in a very quick and harsh manner. There I was in bed! In my head it began spinning. AIDS, AIDS, AIDS.... Suddenly the definite feeling: now I will die. Today, perhaps tomorrow, or the day after tomorrow. Panic broke out. I was stiff, empty, cold, entirely alone, and I believed I was standing in front of death.

When my boyfriend phoned, I told him I was HIV positive. His answer was, " I knew this." I did not want to believe what he said. I thought we had no secrets between us, had trusted each other. Anger rose within me, sadness too. So he had infected me consciously. From that time on I did not want to have any more calls from him. I almost boiled over with hatred, rage, anger and despair. Then, when I wanted to talk with him about this, it was too late. He had taken his life. A cold shiver ran down my spine. I understood nothing anymore.

My hospital release followed. I was certain that I would

be able to go back and stay with my best friend. But when she heard that I was positive, she said she was sorry, but "I had to look out for myself."

Death, which followed me, stressed me to such an extent that often I too contemplated suicide. Everything was dark, I felt lost, so lonely and without support. Finally I moved in with a family which was friendly, maybe just out of pity. There I felt a little happiness because I liked the three children so very much. But happiness turned to hell. Separate toilets, separate laundry, separate sleeping corners, no little kisses for the children. Each AIDS newspaper and magazine article was held under my nose. I felt completely written off, did not know how to relate any of that stuff to myself, except that I saw death. Then nightmares where the bed vibrated and someone screamed "AIDS!" non-stop.

My solitude increased rapidly. The days were long, empty, wretched, lifeless, senseless, dark. AIDS, AIDS, AIDS, death, death, death. I was like a piece of stone, an icicle. Soon I drank continuously to turn off. But the awakening was terrifying.

One day a woman dragged me to an AIDS support group. At first I was shocked. So many people, and almost everyone looked healthy and alert. The thought, "they are just like me," shot through my head. On that same evening, for the first time, I didn't feel alone anymore. There are so many others who are in the same boat. Somehow life has to continue. I then went to the group on a regular basis. As time went by, I began to work again and got my own apartment.

In the beginning, it went very well. But then I could not bear my spare time and the "loneliness" anymore without drugs and alcohol. AIDS and doubt overtook me again. I took alcohol and drugs blindly, until I couldn't cope anymore and I attempted suicide. I woke up again in hospital.

From there, to the psychiatrist. I talked about AIDS, my fears, doubts. Suddenly I wanted to know everything about this illness. I devoured reports, articles, brochures, simply everything I could find. I discovered that I am not sick at all, but for the time being am only HIV positive. I began to think, until I slowly realized that I can live many more years. To be HIV positive is no immediate death sentence, and AIDS and HIV positive are not at all the same. After a general check-up, I left hospital as a healthy being. I could hardly believe this and felt suddenly elated with my future. How to continue now?

I married a gay man. At first it was a good feeling to have a home again, to live with someone who needed me as much as I needed him. But after a certain time this was not enough for me, because I was there only to mix his drugs, earn money and nurture him. I was on my feet around the clock. Then I began to shoot drugs. After five months, I couldn't stand it anymore. Emotionally I collapsed. After withdrawal, I reached my lowest point. For a few days, nobody could talk to me and I stood in front of a picture; it was of one white door (life) and a black door (death). Luckily I decided for the white. A light came and a pleasant feeling flowed through me. Today after exactly two years, I stand differently in the world.

I am trying to live soberly, indeed consciously. I want to listen to my body, take it seriously. Also, I experience nature as something quite different. I eat more consciously, and attempt to come to terms with myself. Also, I have met people whom I can trust again.

My catchnet is people who mean a lot to me, where I am accepted as I am, where I can knock whenever and in whatever state I am. That for me is a calming, necessary, helpful support, which I know how to protect. Also, the support group has become very important. My goal is to find a "healthy" frame for my life, such as work that I like. Essential for me is to be able to talk openly about being HIV positive. It belongs to me like my feet, my hands. It has become an important part of me.

MARIA

HUNGARY

*Like Nicole in the previous piece, Maria talks of her
unhappy childhood and her estranged relationship with
her parents. Whereas Nicole discovered a way out of her
unhappiness, Maria's depression is constant.*

*Finding out she is HIV positive was a tragedy in
the midst of a life filled with disappointment and fail-
ure. The result of this is that Maria's HIV diagnosis
doesn't seem to make a great deal of difference to her. If
anything, it alleviates the dilemma of planning for the
future.*

*Despite Maria's bleak outlook, she speaks very open-
ly and articulately about HIV in a way that many people living with this disease are afraid to do.*

*Maria is a founding member of PLUSS, the
Hungarian Society of HIV Positive Persons. Her story
is adapted from an interview with Dr. Denes Banhegyi
who works with PLUSS.*

My parents got divorced in 1980 after a 20-year marriage. This did not surprise me. It surprised me a lot more that the marriage lasted so long, as emotionally my mother and father had nothing in common. Emotions did not exist in our family. My father was not interested in family life. I think he loved me when I was a child. But when I was six or seven, he didn't care for me anymore, perhaps because I was a helpless child and he did not like that. He wanted a quick-witted daughter.

We don't see each other, unless I go to see my grandmother who lives at his place. She is the only emotional person in the family, the only one who loved me in her own way. She is rather an aggressive and haughty woman, but she liked me, I guess.

My mother looked after me and my brother. She gave us what we needed, but that was all. And when I was 18, she stopped taking care of me. Then I had to look after myself. She must have thought she had fulfilled her duty, brought me up, and the rest of it was none of her business. But to tell the truth, I have no idea of why she acted like this. It was impossible to talk about things like that with her. Even if she happened to listen to my questions, she never answered them, but withdrew into herself as if offended. At these times she most probably labelled me as one of her enemies. She always went on at great length about how ungrateful people were and how much injustice she had to suffer day by day. She, of course, never made mistakes. If anything went wrong, it was always somebody else's fault or wickedness. And sooner or later she found someone to blame on. As long as I was a child and dependent on her, she was a loving mother. But when I was in my teens she became estranged from me, convinced I had changed for the worse. I offended her. I don't know what she was thinking about because I behaved like an ordinary teenager. There was nothing abnormal in my behaviour.

I absorbed her coldness. I have taken it with me. I became lonely. I was not loud or funny. I had nothing special in me that attracted people. No one accepted me in their company though I wanted to go out with them. I went to school with the same people for eight years, but I had only one friend during this time. And the same thing happened in high school. I had no other friends there. I didn't do well at school. I had a lot of trouble and was never able to listen attentively. I had no particular interest in anything. I only went to high school because my mother wanted me to. I had a boy friend and tried to become accepted in his circle, but I just remained an outsider and before the final exam he left me for another girl. We both felt everything had gone wrong between us, so I told him to do as he pleased.

After I graduated I had to go to work, but I didn't know what job I could do. I was not particularly interested in anything. I changed jobs often. I worked in a library, in a factory, as a dispatcher, a paper girl, and in a kindergarten. I had the feeling I was alone in the world. I had no friends that I chose. If somebody picked me as their friend, we went out together. But when I initiated something it always fell through. I am not assertive. I don't want to force myself on anybody and my attempts came to nothing. So I have never been the chooser.

I don't bother about who infected me. There is nothing I can do about it. Perhaps it was a foreign student from Africa. He left for home a long time ago. There is nobody else I can put my finger on. It's a long time back. AIDS was hardly known at that time. It never occurred to me that I could be infected.

One day I fell ill. I thought I had the flu. It got worse and worse and my hands and feet started to become numb. There was absolutely no feeling in them. This happened in less than five days. I couldn't sleep, I was so nervous. I finally went to see the district doctor who prescribed some aspirin – in other words he did not take it seriously. But later as I became progressively worse, he became suspicious. By the time he sent me to hospital, I could hardly move. I was put into the intensive care unit because they were scared. They thought my lungs would go numb and I would have to go on artificial respiration. They gave me sleeping pills and finally I was able to sleep. When they saw I could breathe normally, they transferred me to the Neurological Department to treat me. It was there that they discovered that I was HIV positive.

A week or so later they sent me to the Laszlo Hospital for an examination. I was surprised because I started feeling better and even was able to stand when holding on to something. At first, they didn't tell me what was wrong with me. It was only two weeks later that they told me why they had taken me to Laszlo Hospital. When they told me that I was HIV positive, I went into absolute shock. What shall I do now? How can I live? And for how long? What will my life be like? Will I ever have a boyfriend again? I thought things could not possibly get better, so I might as well kill myself. Why should I suffer to the end?

For several months I was not able to think about anything but AIDS. Only my body was present at work; my thoughts were far away. Then I met a boy. This made me even more worried. Can I go out with boys at all? At first I acted as though I had no interest in the relationship. I had no courage to tell him that I had AIDS. If I tell him, he will leave me right away and if he leaves me right away, why should I tell him? I tried to protect him from getting the virus in every possible way. For a time, it was tough because he refused to use condoms. But I kept on talking him into it and in the end I succeeded.

However he didn't always use one. I became sick and tired of everything and took all the sedatives and sleeping pills I had at home. I was discovered and saved. The boy came to see me in the hospital. I was very depressed. I couldn't get rid of the thought that I can never have a good time in life. After I got out of the hospital, we went out together again, but after a while he left me. Not because he learnt that I was ill but because our relationship went wrong. It was better than if he had left me because I had AIDS. In the end, I didn't tell him.

For about six months I felt really low. Why should I live? Then I felt a little better. Why should I panic in advance, I thought. I kept thinking about my illness. I was not afraid of death but of suffering. It doesn't bother me that I shall die. But I'm scared of lying helplessly in bed and waiting for somebody to take care of me. That would be terrible.

I told my mother that I was HIV positive. She asked me not to tell anyone else and I agreed. I had told a girlfriend and she turned her back on me. She didn't say our friendship was over, but she looked very much afraid of me and she didn't know what to say. At the same time, she was curious and wanted to know many things about the illness and what the homosexual men are like at PLUSS (the Hungarian society of HIV Positive Persons). Her curiosity was natural but she was not at all interested in me and in my sorrows.

I don't mind being mostly with homosexuals; it's of secondary importance. The point is that they are also ill with the same problems. These fears cannot be shared with anybody else. Those who are not concerned won't understand it. We'd better not try to be open with them. Here I can tell my problems.

Since I fell ill I have been living in another world. Healthy people won't enter this world. They speculate over their future, planning and day-dreaming. I, however, can speculate over AIDS, and that's all. There is no point in planning anything for the future, given the illness can shove in its oar at any time. I may be wrong. You should have your aims in life when you are not ill. But I have never been a person who knows what I am after. Now I work at home. I am employed in my mother's business. I am not having a good time. I wish I could leave home. I have to find a job. That's my only purpose now.

My mother is not interested in AIDS. Once when I spoke to her in detail about AIDS, she told me off saying I shouldn't complain as her life is a lot harder than mine. We have never said a word about my illness ever since. What's more, my family talks about things due to happen in ten years' time as if I will take part in them as a matter of course: What's going to happen when I get married? How are we going to sell the house, and all the rest of it. These are not my plans, of course, and at these times I don't say a word. These are their plans. My mother pretends as if my illness were nobody's concern. And I really don't want to talk about it with her any more either, even if she wanted to. With other people, yes. At PLUSS I don't feel like a stranger, as if no such disease existed, as if it existed only in my fantasy.

I know this disease exists and that I can die of it. But as there was nobody that I could talk with about it, I felt as lonely as a stray man from Mars. When I started to talk about AIDS with other people, they looked at me as if I were a freak or a monster in a fairy tale – absolutely astonished. I should add that my mother has always thought of me as a daydreamer. She was not receptive to my emotional problems in my adolescence. When I was depressed for weeks on end, she told me that I was trying to make everybody feel sorry for me, that I blamed others and bothered them with my troubles. She said that if I wanted to I could leave my depression behind. She kept on hammering things like that into me, so much that I thought AIDS was one of those imagined diseases, until I met some other people who had AIDS. At least, my mother cannot say it does not exist.

People I know don't know that I have AIDS. They think AIDS is exclusively a disease of homosexuals. They make dirty jokes about it. Once, for example, there was a disgusting bottle lying somewhere, mouldy and grimy. Suddenly someone said, "Put this AIDS bottle away."

In their fantasies people are concerned about AIDS, but they rarely talk about it. They don't think they are in danger. They most probably believe that respectful and educated people like them cannot get it, as if it were a disease for the lower classes. If they happen to walk under a disgusting underpass, they might think, well, this is the place where you can get it. All in all, AIDS is no concern of theirs. Many times I have pictured it in my mind what they would say if I told them I had AIDS. It would certainly throw them into panic.

I am not surprised by their behaviour. People do not talk about what they are afraid of. It's not true only of AIDS. If, for instance, they want to get married, they are liable to forget about their partner's bad habits with great compassion. The trouble is that they have to face it later on. And if they get into trouble, they think they have nothing to do with it. And then they become confused. Like my girlfriend that I have known for 18 years and who has not been able to be straightforward with me ever since I told her that I have AIDS. I didn't think she would behave like this. Sure, I would be confused too. I would not be able to put myself in another person's position, but I think I wouldn't be so scared. I have become accustomed to the thought of AIDS. The virus carriers also hate it and are afraid of it.

I am different. Most HIV positive people were more determined before they got the disease. They had plans and goals that were ruined by the disease. I was not a very ambitious person even before my disease. I had no major goals that were ruined by AIDS. There are moments when I even feel happy. I don't have to bother about my future since now I know what's going to happen. It may sound silly, but I have been suffering so much from being uncertain about things. I have always been worried about how to manage in life, how to become independent. Now it is not so tragic anymore. I don't have to sort my whole life out, only one or two years.

I often thought I would kill myself. Why should a helpless freak survive? Somebody who has no plans to carry out? But I have never done it. When I tried to commit suicide, I thought I had enough good reasons to put an end to all this. When they saved my life, first it left me indifferent. But then I thought many times how good it would have been if I had succeeded. But now it doesn't matter. I'll wait it out.

BARBARA EMES
USA

Barbara Emes describes herself: "I am a 32 year old PWA (Person with AIDS). I live on a farm in a small town in Pennsylvania. I was diagnosed HIV positive six years ago. I have three children, Noah, 13, Becca, 9, and Christian, 8. I was married last year. About six months ago I went public with my diagnosis. Since then I have been on TV and in the newspaper. I have given many speeches, became a buddy to another HIV positive woman and am a member of several advisory committees for our local AIDS project. I am in the process of starting a local ACT-UP group in my area. My life has improved so much, because I'm learning to nurture myself for the first time.

I hope that these photos will show that a PWA is much more than just a Person with AIDS. We are daughters, mothers, wives, lovers, activists. We have moments of joy and ecstacy and also sadness and fear. We have moments of strength and moments of vulnerability. We laugh, we cry, we live – just like everyone else."

– *Daryl Emes*

1. BARBARA IN THE YARD. WE MOVED TO THE COUNTRY FOR PRIVACY AND A HEALING ATMOSPHERE AFTER MY DIAGNOSIS. 2. BARBARA, THREE MONTHS OLD. 3. IN THE BAHAMAS ON MY THIRTIETH BIRTHDAY. 4. DARYL AND BARBARA GETTING MARRIED, OCTOBER 20, 1990. 5. SEXUALITY IS AS IMPORTANT AS EVER. 6. NAPS ARE NOW JUST PART OF THE DAILY ROUTINE.

1. ENTRANCE, NATIONAL INSTITUTES OF HEALTH. WE MAKE THIS TWO-HOUR TRIP WEEKLY FOR A CLINICAL DRUG TRIAL. 2. BEING IN THE CLINICAL TRIAL FOR THE L-DRUG. I HAVE TO HAVE ONE PINT OF BLOOD TAKEN EVERY WEEK. 3. BARBARA'S MASK MADE BY RICK, HER MEDICINE MAN. 4. TAKING MY EXPERIMENTAL DRUG FOR THE FIRST TIME: REAL OR PLACEBO?

— Daryl Emes

5. BEGINNING A HERBAL CLEANSING FAST. NO FOOD FOR SIX DAYS. T4 CELLS ROSE BY 100 FOLLOWING THE CLEANSE. 6. FIRST BOTTLE OF HOMEMADE HERBAL MEDICINE, "PLANETARY BITTERS CURE ALL." THE RECIPE CAME FROM OLD NATIVE AMERICAN MEDICINE MAN IN THE APPALACIAN MOUNTAINS.

– Daryl Emes

1. MILITANT MOM AND DAUGHTER; BECCA, AGE 9 ON RIGHT. 2. BARBARA READING NAMES AT NAME'S PROJECT QUILT DISPLAY, ALLENTOWN, PA. 3. BEING INTERVIEWED AT AN ACT-UP DEMONSTRATION. 4. BARBARA STARTED LANCASTER AREA ACT-UP. FIRST MEETING AT HER HOUSE. 5. ACT-UP DEMONSTRATION. 6. WE TIED RIBBONS ALL OVER OUR COUNTRY AS PART OF ACT-UP'S NATION-WIDE PINK RIBBON CAMPAIGN. THEY HONOUR THOSE DEAD FROM AIDS AND SIGNIFY HOPE AND SUPPORT FOR THOSE OF US STILL LIVING WITH AIDS.

PAMELA BLANEY
CANADA

Pamela lives in Western Canada. She describes the loneliness and reclusiveness that took over her life when she was told that she was HIV positive. Suddenly, her contact with the outside world became limited to doctor's appointments. She also talks about the difficulty of finding supportive health care for HIV positive people.

After a long period of complete isolation, Pamela is now active with the Winnipeg Body Positive Group, an organization for people living with AIDS.

In the summer of 1984, a public health nurse notified me that I had been involved with a person who was infected with HIV and I had to be tested. For three months every Tuesday I went to the Health Science Centre for tests. Dr C also felt it would be a good idea for my six-year-old daughter to be tested. Better to be safe than sorry. The worst part of the whole testing was how dirty I felt. Each time my blood was taken, a yellow sticker saying "Warning: Dangerous Fluids" was put on every tube.

My results were finalized one week before my thirtieth birthday. I was positive, my daughter was negative. From that moment on, I considered that death could happen at anytime.

Not much of a birthday present, for not only was my health in limbo, I lost a number of important things in my life. I cut myself off from friends and my social life. Basically, my life as I knew it gradually disappeared. My phone number became unlisted, and I screened all of my calls. I no longer went clothes shopping but would get everything I needed through Eatons and The Bay's "Buy Line." A nanny was hired and my daughter went there everyday after school. I did still have to go grocery shopping, but I changed stores for fear of bumping into anyone I knew.

I also continued to see Dr C. I became quite trusting and dependent on him. I did what he recommended medically and even had an abortion when we found out I was pregnant along with the HIV test result. This happened so fast I never even had time to grieve. Today I still would have had an abortion, but I might have thought a bit more about it.

Dr. C felt that my family should know. My family doctor tried to explain it to my father. He listened but would not accept what the doctor said. Perhaps one day he will accept, or at least understand.

Dr. C figured the only possible way I could have contacted the disease was when I was raped in late March. It was a form of date rape. Forced sodomy was not something I had experienced before.

I started to have very bad luck with doctors. First, in the summer of 1985, Dr C took a position in Kenya. My holistic doctor, Dr S, lost his licence and decided to move. I still keep in contact with him and he phones a couple of times a year, sends me information and sees me when he is in town.

I continued to go to my family doctor. But unfortunately he did not feel he was the right medical person to treat me, although he would always be there as a friend or for emergencies. He had enquired about the Village Clinic where a lot of HIV positive people get health services and asked if I would be willing to go there. At the Clinic, I met a counsellor, Dennis, who worked very hard to make me feel comfortable. He educated me about what the virus does to my body, what to be careful about, and what is dangerous.

At this point my social life consisted of seeing Dennis once a week, and the doctor every six weeks. Again in the fall of 1989, Dr. E, my new doctor at the Village Clinic, left.

I had been going to the Clinic for about a year and with each visit I felt a bit more secure. My major mistake at that time is that I enrolled in a drug trial and became ill. But the idea that I was dirty or I had done something wrong was diminishing. I was a woman who needed medical and psychological help. I really appreciate the help the doctors and counsellors gave me. I began to see Dr. S at the Clinic, who so far has stayed.

I became very tired of being alone with my daughter. I missed having a social life. People really do not know how easy it is to become a hermit. But coming back into society is hard. My closest friend could not understand why he did not hear from me. When I explained what was happening to me a definite stress was put on our relationship until he found out more about HIV. Today I am happy to say we are still very close friends.

I have rekindled other friendships. But I did make one mistake, telling a girl I went to school with. She is a nurse and took it upon herself to contact my daughter's dentist. The dentist phoned me and asked me to come in, so I did. He asked me to verify the story. He was my daughter's dentist and not mine, yet he charged me over a hundred dollars for this so-called consultation. I terminated his services. I went to Dennis who helped me report the nurse through the right channels. Today we do not talk, but I guess it was not a real friendship.

During 1988, I found I was slowing down. I didn't seem to have much energy. Even though I worked in a family business I had to stop working. This was the first time in my life I actually had to be careful with money. Today I live on Canada Disability Pension and I am thankful for that.

The past year has been very affirmative, though not perfect. I try to get out at least once a week with my friends. I go shopping without fear of people realizing I am carrying the disease. I am making new friends, travelling, and I'm not afraid of people.

Today I realize that my body doesn't have the black plague. The other night I went to a hockey game with a friend. He introduced me to an actor who worked on an AIDS play. We talked about HIV and AIDS. He said he felt how rough it must be for anyone who had HIV or AIDS. I said I tested positive, but I was not afraid.

—JAE

BEV

AUSTRALIA

Bev is active internationally as a spokesperson for women living with HIV and AIDS. She is the co-founder of Positive Women, *a self-help group for women living with HIV and AIDS in Melbourne, Australia.*

Bev is also a welfare worker, mother and wife of an HIV positive man. They met and married after their diagnoses.

This piece has been adapted from two speeches Bev has given at conferences. She speaks about the difficulties of being an HIV positive woman living in a country where AIDS has largely affected the gay community. HIV positive women are too often stereotyped as prostitutes, junkies, "vectors of transmission" or innocent victims. Bev challenges those involved in AIDS work in Australia to recognize that women get AIDS and to integrate women into the AIDS dialogue.

I was diagnosed HIV positive in late 1984 after I was informed that my partner's ex-lover died of AIDS. My initial reaction was incredible shock, disbelief and anger. Why me? I had been in a monogamous relationship for years! Did women get it? Will I die? My doctor at the time said that this meant I would probably be dead within three years.

In my stubbornness, I refused to accept this death sentence and set about to find out information, and to receive treatment and support.

Seeking support, I told all my friends, who were generally very supportive, although there were some people who disappeared out of my life. I am unsure what they have done with the precious information I entrusted to them.

Eventually, I did contact the AIDS Council of Melbourne. I was asked "Did you get it from work, luvvie?" Generally, while the various AIDS-related agencies assisted me, I was seen as an oddity.

I felt incredibly lonely and isolated. In my need for support from other positive people, I joined *Positive Friends* in 1985 where I was the only woman amongst gay men. In this support group, I was seen as "one of the boys." Although flattering, this did not address my specific needs and concerns of being a positive woman. I left the group after a year.

I yearned to meet other positive women and asked my new doctor about other women. I was told yes, there are other women, but we were too diverse to jell as a group.

It was not until 1988 — three-and-a-half years after my diagnosis — that I met another positive woman. At our first meeting, we found we had similar experiences, concerns and needs. We had both experienced an incredible lack of services sensitive to women's needs. We also found there was minimal information about women with HIV. It was pretty easy to pick up a brochure about AIDS or even one about safe sex; but none, even now, address the implications for women with HIV, and how to deal with it.

Being single heterosexual women, we were concerned about rejection by men when we disclosed our status. Were we to live lonely, isolated, asexual lives? Should we tell and risk rejection, abuse, breaches of confidentiality? Should we forget about relationships and sex altogether? How infectious are we?

At this initial meeting, we decided to form a self-help support group for all women with HIV. This group grew into *Positive Women*, a group which provides mutual support, regular meetings and person-to-person or telephone contact. We give each other support and hope, and we educate public and government about our existence as HIV positive women and the urgency of our needs.

The issues for HIV positive women that were uppermost when *Positive Women* was formed are much the same as the issues for HIV positive women now. They are:

• Little account is taken of the fact that women are still the major nurturers in society and that many infected women still have to fulfil this role in relation to their children and partners, often to the detriment of their own health.

• Infected women are often poor and badly resourced generally which makes them least able to adjust to the problems of HIV infection.

• Women are still marginalized or socially isolated, and thus have had minimal access to appropriate welfare programs.

• Positive women are capable of organizing and maintaining our own self-help groups and networks and do not need to be controlled by men.

• Positive women lack organizational funding. We don't want to be subsidiaries of male-dominated organizations with different priorities to our own.

• Positive women have the right to accurate up-to-date information particularly in the area of reproductive health. Where this information is not available, we have the right to have these questions made an immediate priority of new research programs.

• Positive women should not be seen as vectors of disease nor should they be constituted morally unacceptable because of infection.

• All women require accurate and unbiased information concerning their risk of infection.

• Above all, positive women demand the right to appropriate women-sensitive services. We also demand to be fully involved in AIDS policy development and formation.

REBECCA BLOOMSFIELD
CANADA

Rebecca met her husband Garry at a restaurant where they both worked. Even before discovering that they were both HIV positive, tragedy entered their lives when their son Kevin died shortly after his birth. However they went on to have a daughter, Laura. Later, Garry came down with pneumonia and was admitted to hospital. It was here that he was diagnosed as having AIDS. Rebecca and Laura were subsequently tested for HIV. Rebecca tested positive and Laura tested negative.

Garry's health failed rapidly. Rebecca quickly learnt to become a caregiver when he lost his sight to an AIDS-related illness, CMV retinitis. During this nightmare of pressure, responsibility and uncertainty, Rebecca began to keep a journal for the first time in her life. She developed an intimate rapport with her typewriter which she often addresses as "my friend." One of Rebecca's dreams is to see her journal published. Her other dreams for her future are illustrated in her drawings that accompany this piece.

June 1

Well, it is now 9:30 pm and once again Garry has gone to bed before me, feeling really tired, the way he usually feels except for when he gets his burst of energy. That only lasts for about a couple of days at a time, but then that's the man that I used to know. I saw him one day as we were on our way to Sunnybrook Hospital. I saw him sitting in the bus shelter, staying away from the sun because, you see, it's important that he stays away from the sun rays. As I was casually looking over at him, he looked too tired to take any more of this bullshit that he has been going through since this whole episode began last year. It just seems like the hospital and the doctors are running our lives as well as the social workers.

But I think that this whole ordeal has really been going on since 1980 when he started feeling something strange going on with his body. He said he had a touch of pneumonia back then and some night sweats as well. Ever since 1988, he had the same symptoms and still didn't know what it was, until I had him admitted into Toronto East General Hospital at the end of February. When he was admitted all the doctor told me was that he had a bad case of pneumonia and a yeast infection in his mouth and in his throat. But they still didn't know what was causing severe diarrhea and a massive weight loss. He went from 160 pounds to about 124 pounds within a three to four month period. After many tests, they finally told him that he had AIDS. He phoned me at home and said that they had finally told him why he was losing all this weight. He said to me, "You will never guess what they told me was wrong with me. You will never guess what it is in a million years." And I had said "What?" out of excitement. "I have found out that I have AIDS." And I said, "WHAT? I can't believe it." All I could think about is "How dare you give it to me?"

I guess Garry feels that he could kill the person who gave it to him. He was trying to make a new life with a woman whom he loves dearly and who had a beautiful son who never had a chance at life. But he knows that he has a beautiful daughter whom he thinks the world of. I can never forget the look on his face when he saw Laura come into the world. He had a beautiful look on his face and tears in his eyes saying, "Finally God has allowed us to have at least one child."

Once we were over the shock of knowing, we tried to reach out to people who knew about the disease and that is how we learned about ACT (AIDS Committee of Toronto). I can remember the first time that Garry and I went there we were told to meet with a counsellor named Marie Robertson. The first time that we met her she welcomed us with open arms. I don't just mean with words. I mean she actually gave us both big hugs. And that's something that I've really gotten accustomed to in the past year from people I know who are associated with AIDS. I would like to tell everyone that if you know someone who has AIDS, please give them a big hug, because that's something that they really need right now in their life. It makes them feel that they are not contagious if you just give them a hug.

Recently Garry told me that his right eye, which was just blurry, was gone. What I mean by "gone" is that he can only see shadows with bright light behind them. The doctor has warned him in the past that if his white cell count doesn't come back up, that they can't put him on the Foscarnet anymore. All they can do is give him an antibiotic for his eyes. That would mean letting nature take its course, meaning letting his eyes go blind. But he will still be able to see light and some shadows. And you know, I think that is where Garry is headed because of the way he is feeling these days.

He seems to be more run down. He seems to be coughing a lot which keeps him awake at nights and he has had to sleep on the couch for the past few nights. It's been sort of nice having the bed to myself, but on the other hand I miss having his nice warm body to cuddle up with at night.

June 7

When I was told by my husband that he had AIDS I said that I hated him and that was not true. At that point, I didn't know that I had the virus. But after I had found out from the doctor that I was HIV positive, that is when I started to hate him. Many people asked me if I were going to leave him because of his sickness. I said no because I love him and I could never leave him. When you have been married as long as we have and had all the trouble we have had in the past, this really makes you a lot closer.

June 15

Well, hello, my friend. It's me again. I didn't think I would be talking to you tonight. But I feel that I must because I am going through a lot of heavy emotions in the past few days. After tonight at my support group, I feel I must talk to you, even though I should be in bed. Well for starters, I have been trying to be strong for Garry, since he has now gone blind in the past few days. I have been his eyes lately and he is really depending on me. In the past few days, he is really trying to reach out for me. Just when I thought that he didn't want to give me any affection while he is trying to deal with his sickness. And with dealing with this sickness, you seem to lose your desire to have sex with your partner. But just recently he did make some movements towards me. Even though it was only half way, it was still something and that made me feel really good inside. It almost made me feel like a whole woman again.

Tonight was the first time that I have had to deal with my emotions since the blindness has come to Garry. I had what you might call a little bit of a breakdown. But I must say that I did feel better after my check-in with the group. What I mean by a "check-in" is that you have to tell how you are feeling for the week and what has been happening with your life since the last time you were at the group. I never thought I would be that vulnerable in front of all the girls, but, you know, it doesn't seem to bother me any more. They have pretty much become part of my life in the past year. I guess it will be a year in November, since I have been going to my support group for HIV positive women. I need this group every week, because it feels good to have something to rely on for support.

June 20

I went to Sunnybrook Hospital to see Garry. I was feeling pretty good at that point, because I had had a nice bus ride. When I arrived at the hospital, I proceeded to the D4 Wing where Garry is. Seeing him again started to depress me because he doesn't look good at all right now. We did manage to go for a little walk to the Harvest Room for a soft drink. But we didn't stay long because he started to get cold again. So we went back to his room, where he returned to his bed all curled up in his blankets. He wasn't really much company this time. Usually he is able to sit up more and we go for walks and then he makes us a cup of coffee and we sit and chat together. But it was nothing like that at all, so I decided to watch TV until Dr. Rachlis came up to the floor and made her rounds.

When she came to Garry's room, she checked him over and asked what was wrong with him. Once she finished the examination, she told us that he has standard pneumonia and the reason that he had probably got it was from his white cell count being so low. She really didn't want to say much until his tests were complete. I said, "All I want is to see him better, a little better than he is." She said, "We are trying our best right now and we only have a certain amount of drugs to work with." It puzzled me when she said that. I worried that she had taken me the wrong way. So after I said good-bye to Garry and noticed that she was still there at the nurses' desk, I confronted her and said, "I hope you didn't take me the wrong way when I said that I would like to see him better. I wasn't judging your ability." And she said, "Yes, I know what you meant." She added one thing that she didn't say in front of Garry, that he is getting worse instead of better. Not to say that he is on death's doorstep, but things are going in that direction. And I know she was telling the truth, because she had always said he was doing great; he was on hold.

So when I went to my group tonight, I didn't think that I could handle being there after what was told to me. But instead I got a few things off my chest. I am really looking forward to my visit with my counsellor Marie on Thursday, because I think that I will probably really hang loose with her. I talk about my problems living with a person who has AIDS. But I feel that I am right back where I was three years ago when I was watching my baby die and now I am watching my own husband die. I guess the thing that is most hard to deal with is the waiting. How do you know how to prepare yourself because you never know when it will happen. When it does happen, it really hurts like hell. Even now, just talking about it makes me sick inside.

June 21

Well, good morning, my friend. I managed to have a relatively good night's sleep. I didn't think that I would because of what was told to me yesterday. So this morning I took Laura to the sitter's place and then I went to the donut shop and sat there and enjoyed the view out the window. I guess you can call it my moment of peace and quiet.

I had better tell you about the dream that I had a couple of nights ago. It is one of those dreams that sticks in your mind and you can't seem to get rid of the thought. One part of the dream was about death. The people that I saw dead in this dream were my mother and my Uncle Jim and my Aunt Beatrice. Another part was about a party with all my sister's friends and they were celebrating some kind of reunion. My sister wasn't at this party, being in Australia. Then the most gorey part of this dream was when I thought that I was trimming a fish. To my surprise it was actually a seal, a full grown one. That really freaked me out. Then I remembered seeing some person all covered with blood from the waist down. I remember that I carried the head, and another person carried the body downstairs to the basement of my parents' place. That is when the dream ended because at that point the alarm went off at 7:00 am. And for some reason, this dream is still sticking in my mind. Maybe it has something to do with Garry. Who knows?

Next week at group, we have to tell what we had drawn on the piece of paper that they had given us. The idea is they

"GRAVESITE"

Finally
No more
trips
to SunnyBrook
Hospital

Friends
& Family Around

For Support

LAURA'S
graduation

"1990 Mommy Cure of Aids"

I am finally cured
of Aids

LAURA & Husband
Expecting first Baby

Grandmother

Plenty of New Friends

My Graduation from Business School

Telephone computer

My New Career

First House

Resting in Peace Knowing that I AM going to Be alright

Parents

Husband

Get Married once again.

"This time for ever"

want us to see what we think our lives will be like two years from now. It can be words or pictures of different pieces of our lives. And what I drew was, I guess, sort of negative thoughts and some positive thoughts. The negative thoughts were seeing Laura, myself, and Garry standing there as a family and also in the picture of the family, you can see Garry with a cane in his hand. Then there was a scene with Laura and I standing over the gravesite of Garry with all our friends around us. And even afterwards there were lots of friends around us after the death. Then there was a scene with Laura and I together watching her grow up. And there were the words: "Finally no more trips to Sunnybrook Hospital." Then one other statement: "Mommie cured of AIDS." So I think subconsciously this picture had an effect on my life in some way because of what had happened yesterday. It could be just a coincidence but who knows?

I am having a lot of mixed feelings right now. I don't know what I am supposed to be feeling. I don't know if I should start planning a funeral, or just take one day at a time as I have been doing in the past year, or I should say, in the past few years, ever since I moved in with Garry. And, you know, I can remember the day that I moved in with Garry. It was a great day because when I got there Garry had turned on the stereo and had played the song by Roberta Flack called "The First Time Ever I Saw Your Face." And then we danced to it and I started to cry. And sometimes I wish that I could have that day back again, because I know that I would fall in love even more with Garry.

A month or so before I moved in with Garry, he had asked me to go out with him. And that night was so beautiful. In the evening we had seen a movie. Afterwards, we went to a bar at the Carlton Inn Hotel. We had been tossing the idea around as to whether or not our relationship would work and whether Garry could change from being gay to going straight so he could be with me. It finally worked out well because at the end of the evening we managed to polish off four half-litres of white wine so we were feeling no pain. And as we were leaving to go home, we stopped in one spot and started to kiss each other. It wasn't just a little kiss. It was a passion kiss. At that point I knew it was official that we were going with each other. I guess I am reminiscing. But right now I wish that we were back at this point in our lives instead of where we are now, our life being invaded with this damn disease AIDS. I guess I had better bring myself back to the real world.

June 27

One thing that I am not looking forward to is telling Laura the truth about her daddy dying of AIDS. Or should I just lie and say that he died of cancer? When she starts school and makes friends, they might question her about where her father is. And how could she tell her friends that her daddy had died of AIDS? And this would be with the heterosexual people who are not very supportive of us.

I'm not saying that all people are prejudiced, because so far I haven't run into anybody, except my family physician who I have had since I was a baby. He said that it was best that I should see another doctor who knows about AIDS and how to treat it. But he was actually saying that it was Garry's fault, that he got this by sleeping with other men. These aren't the exact words of the doctor, but this is the picture that he painted for us. One day before I had stopped seeing him – I was still getting allergy shots at that time and I had gone to him occasionally for the injections – he said, "What are you doing here? Your appointment should have been cancelled." He said that I shouldn't really get shots since I am infected with the HIV. I left the office with tears in my eyes. How could he do this to me after seeing me all these years both as a child and as a woman? After a while I told my counsellor, Marie and she said, "I know of a good GP and I can set an appointment for you if you'd like." I said, "Yes, I would." So ever since last April I have been seeing a great doctor and his name is Dr. Abe Hirsz. Oh, and what a hunk he is! And very gentle with you as well.

Last night I actually had a long talk with Garry about his future and his funeral. I think that he would like to be cremated and have his ashes spread at the waterfront. That place is a special place in our minds. It is a place where you can live in a dream world because the place is wonderful. I also said, "If you'd like, I could arrange to have your urn buried on top of our son Kevin, because it would be small enough to go on top of his grave. All I would have to get is another tombstone." And he said he would like that. So at least he has acknowledged death a little.

I think that you would like to hear the story of Kevin because a lot of good things have come out of that time of my life. I think that it would be good for me to tell this story, because it might help me deal with some feelings that I have for him that affect me during this new crisis in my life. Because I am going through the same sort of things that my husband and I went through together. I am again watching someone that I love very much die, only this time it is a grown man rather than a child. At least I have been given more time with Garry than I had with my son. It's not so bad when an adult dies, because at least they have experienced more life than a child.

I don't know what is wrong with me. As I am typing out my feelings to you, I seem to be always talking about the way things used to be. I'm thinking about my son a lot more these days. Even as I am travelling on the transit system, journeying out somewhere, I find myself thinking about death all the time. Maybe I am thinking, "When is this all going to be all over?" First I had to deal with the death of Kevin. Now I am watching a grown man dying of AIDS, knowing my little girl will grow up without a daddy. I know maybe I will marry again, but how do you tell a man that you have the AIDS virus and that he must wear a latex condom before we make love? I guess everyone is saying that we all hope there will be a cure for AIDS. Once this whole horrifying disease is off the face of the earth I think that everyone, including myself, can have peace of mind. Well, it looks like it will be a good night for sleeping, because there is a cool breeze blowing through the window next to me. You might say that it is my creative light. Well, my friend, I think that I will try and talk to you a bit later. If you don't hear from me in the next couple of days, don't worry because I will probably try and catch up on my letter writing.

August 3

One thing that Marie, my counsellor, was telling me was that I like to type about the past a lot and that I feel the safest talking about the past. You know, that is true because back then I wasn't infected with this damn disease called AIDS. It just seems like my whole life is being run by this damn disease. You know, I am feeling really inspired right now to type on you tonight. You know why? Because I have the radio beside me on and it's playing the song "Endless Love." The song makes me feel real warm inside, remembering what it was like back then. This is the song that Garry and I chose for our first dance on our wedding day four years ago. I only wish that I could have that day back again. We had a lot more friends back then. Those friends we didn't get through AIDS. AIDS was something that you wouldn't bring up at the dinner table. Or ever think that you would get it. Well, my friend, I will have to talk to you later, because I hear my husband giving Laura a bath. This is when I usually make my escape for the store, so Laura doesn't make a fuss when I go out the door. Hopefully I will be able to talk to you some more this evening. So bye for now!

August 11

This may sound odd, but lately I have been feeling angry towards the virus, more so than I was in the beginning. In the beginning, I was mostly angry with Garry for giving me this virus, and angry with the person who had given him the virus as well. But more and more, as each day goes by, I find myself expressing my feelings towards AIDS and the things that relate to AIDS: CMV retinitis, dealing with death, knowing that it could happen at any time. And I think that I have had my share of death: having to watch my first-born child Kevin die in my arms. To have your flesh and blood die in your arms. To feel something warm and beautiful go stone cold. After he died, I knew he could still feel all the love that was in that room that day. Kevin would have been mentally retarded, because the cord was wrapped around his neck twice and, as we know, that cuts off the oxygen to the brain. We couldn't possibly have looked after him financially. It would have probably ended up with us giving him up to The Children's Aid.

It seems like I only want to talk about the past. It sounds like I don't want to move forward, but I do. But how, when you are living with a dying man? Well, my friend, I guess the one thing that I haven't said to you yet is goodnight. So good-bye for now and I will talk to you tomorrow.

August 17

Boy! It does feel good sitting here tonight. I have a cool breeze coming in through the window. It almost feels like fall weather coming around the corner. It's also the kind of weather where you get under the blankets at night and cuddle up with your husband, hoping something will come out of that. But I know it won't happen because I am slowly accepting the fact that my husband has no desire to make love with me. This is not to say that he doesn't show affection towards me, because he does in other ways: by hugging me and kissing. Still sometimes I know that it is not enough, especially when I get frustrated with him and blurt out the words, "Maybe I should hire a male prostitute for some pleasure!" But a few people have suggested to me that maybe I should consider making love to myself. For instance, my counsellor Marie approached me with the idea. It might be all right for her. This may sound like I'm putting her down but I'm not. It's people in general. In the beginning of the group that was something that we discussed and it turned me off drastically. I almost decided to quit the group at that time, but something kept me there. I am still going to the group. You know, talking all about this has made me forget my own troubles for awhile. I guess talking with you makes me feel as if I am trying to reach a friend through my words.

September 7

Today I had a long stroll through our old neighbourhood which made me feel at home again. I even went right past my son's grave without having a visit. I guess I didn't want to put any more stress in my life. Not that I didn't want to spend some time with my son. It's just with all that I have been going through in my life, I didn't want to add any more pressures. Telling you this makes my heart ache, so I guess this is precisely why I didn't go and see him. I will always love my son and I will never forget him.

I also visited my dentist this morning. This was the reason why I was in the area. I told him about Garry and myself and how Garry had lost his eyesight. Also how he had lost it to AIDS. I think that he was very astonished when I had told him. But he was also very concerned about us and how we are managing with the whole ordeal. I also learned that he would never reject me. I feel reassured and will feel comfortable going back to him on a regular basis. Well, my friend, I will have to say good-bye for now because daddy has the little one in pajamas now and I had better head for the store before it gets too late. So good-bye for now and I will try and talk to you tomorow.

September 18

I saw a man today who was blind and the way he was getting

around totally amazed me. It was as if he were sighted. You know, maybe I am expecting too much of Garry, but I think that the CNIB (the Canadian National Institute for the Blind) should get their act together and help Garry get to that point. I know that things take time, but how much longer does one person have to wait? I know they are doing a wonderful job with Garry so far by teaching him how to read Braille. So far he knows more than I do. I think that I had better catch up to him. Because it would be wonderful to be able to communicate with him once again by printing on paper. Maybe we can leave little love notes for each other.

September 29

Today I have had this sudden burst of energy. I went downstairs before coffee and I did the laundry, cleaned up the dishes, then I cleaned out the bird cage. Finally after that, I put up my feet and rested by sitting down in front of the TV set and watching one of our home videos. I had some time to myself while the other ones were sleeping.

I was so tempted to phone up an old friend, but I didn't quite have the courage to do it. I was thinking he will probably ask what my husband does for a living and if I say he doesn't work, then I will have to explain everything or lie to him. I think that I would like to get together some other place rather than in our home. I am hoping to make some new friends someday, but I think that will happen after my husband passes away. Not to say that it couldn't happen before, because I know that it could happen for me. The only reason that I said that it would probably happen after he passes away is because usually good things happen during the times of troubles. Everyone is there for you afterwards and not during. I know this may sound like I'm being negative, but I think that I am talking reality.

October 1

He has been feeling really lousy this week and I am worried about him. I have been wanting to check him into the hospital, but I have been speaking with Dr. Rachlis's nurse Maureen, and she has assured me that it is just the HIV virus spreading and that there is not much that they can do right now, unless things get really bad for him. I hope that it doesn't. Because you know, I think that I am losing him. I don't know how much longer he has to live. I am hoping that he will be around for Christmas, because I want to make this Christmas a special one for everyone, especially Laura and myself. It will be the first time in about two years that I have not worked during Christmas. I am not planning to, even if they ask me. Well, my friend, I am not feeling the greatest at all. My stomach feels really tense right now. I guess it's all the worrying about him. And I know that for a fact, because I have never felt so alone in my life – having him spend the whole day in bed, then having to be content by myself with Laura for the evening. It made me feel like I am already a single mother. In some ways, I am. I have been alone for the past year-and-a-half.

October 9

Well, hello, my friend. It is now October 9 and I must tell you that I am feeling rather sad right now. You see, I have lost my husband. Yesterday he passed away from the damn disease called AIDS. You know it's just not fair at all. I have never felt so alone in my whole life. I figured when you get married that would end the loneliness, but it seems like I am back to square one again. I know that I have his child with me and that will always be a reminder because she looks so much like her daddy. This Thanksgiving has to be the worst one that I have ever experienced. My parents came over for dinner last night and as we were just finishing, I received a call from the hospital saying that my husband had died a few moments ago. At that point, I couldn't talk to the doctor anymore. My mother took the receiver and finished talking to the doctor. I ran into the bedroom and yelled at life saying, "It's not fair! First you take my baby away and now my husband."

At that point all I wanted to do was to go and see Garry. When I reached his room, which was the same room he was in when he had his second bout of pneumonia, he was still warm. As I was hugging his chest, it was still warm and he really didn't look dead. He looked as if he were just sleeping. I still can't believe he is dead. I guess the reality hasn't sunk in yet. You know, I am really glad that I have you as a friend right now because just typing to you has helped me deal with the pain. I know that I will need somebody to talk to.

October 12

Well, friend, I have finally made it through the day of the funeral. It was the most stressful thing that I have ever had to go through in my life, other than doing it for my son. But at least then I had Garry's shoulder to cry on and now I don't. I have his sister here with me, but it's still not quite the same thing. I have to deal with the insurance agent tomorow and also pick up Garry's urn which I think I will keep for a little while, just to have him close to me. I am still planning on having a service at the gravesite soon, so I can bury him on top of our son Kevin, which was something that Garry wanted. I am now wearing Garry's wedding ring which I couldn't bear to give up because it was part of our marriage vows: "Till death do us part." But you know, I have felt more alone in my life than I ever did before. Even when he was alive, he would be there for me, though not completely, meaning he couldn't give himself to me sexually. We were still able to give hugs and kisses to one another, but I missed the passion-type romance that we used to have in the beginning. You know, I am often wondering what my life is going to be like in the future. I wonder if there will ever be another man in my life like Garry was to me. I did ask Garry on one occasion whether or not he would want me to marry again and he said, "Yes, if a man made you happy and was good to Laura, but mostly treated the both of you well." So now it makes me wonder if that will ever happen for me, knowing that I am HIV positive myself. Now that Garry has finally stopped suffering from AIDS, I sometimes feel that AIDS will be out of my life completely. But it never will, because the damned disease is in my own self.

October 23

Well hello, my friend. I'm sorry that I didn't say good-bye the other day, but I had to put my daughter to bed and I couldn't get back to you. I am not really in good shape right now, because I arranged to bury Garry's ashes on the 28th of October and things have gotten a little tense because the cemetery isn't open on Saturday. It has caused a bit of a problem. So I am waiting to hear from the funeral home to see what they can do.

All I want to do is get on with my life and how can I do this with all of these problems arising? Also I think that problems are going to start up with the daycare. I was talking with my ex-babysitter Edna, and she was telling me that things are starting to get a little hot at the daycare. Some people there have seen Garry's death notice in the paper. I guess they noticed I wanted the donations given to the AIDS Committee of Toronto or Casey House Hospice. Sometimes I just felt like taking Laura and moving out of Toronto, but I guess whereever you move trouble will be sure to follow.

I did manage to get my hair cut and highlighted which made me feel good. Also I didn't have to mention anything about Garry, and I was surprised because usually when you talk to your hairdresser you tell them everything. There will be other people whom I will have to face as well. Well, my friend, the funeral home did call back and everything is confirmed for Saturday. What a relief that is!

October 27

I feel sometimes when I fiddle with my wedding rings, as if I should take them off. But I am scared to because it might seem as though I have given up on the marriage. I still feel as if I am married, having Laura as my proof. When I look at another mother, I look to see if she is wearing a wedding ring and sometimes she doesn't have any ring on at all. So that makes me think that she is a single mother. Mainly I think, "How does she manage raising a child by herself?" I feel that I am in that position now, not having a husband at all.

THE AIDS SUPPORT
ORGANIZATION
(TASO)

UGANDA

TASO was founded in 1987 as the first organized community response to AIDS in Uganda. TASO recognizes that people with HIV and AIDS need support. It now provides over 2,000 people living with HIV and AIDS, as well as their families, with counselling, medical care and material assistance.

What follows is a photo essay depicting the various activities of TASO and people involved in the organization, as well as a written description of the Day Centre by Cate, a young woman client.

1. NOERINE KALEEBA, DIRECTOR OF TASO,
   LOVINGLY KNOWN AS MAMA TASO, AND
   HER ASSISTANT MARBLE MAGEZI
2. MARGARET, YOGA ENTHUSIAST
3. DAY CENTRE'S SEWING WORKSHOP
4. HOME VISIT, DELIVERING FOOD

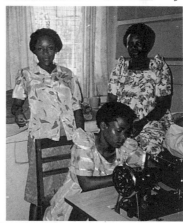

WORLD AIDS DAY 1990 – TASO'S QUILT AND MEMORIAL CELEBRATIONS

I received a warm welcome and cheerful faces greeted me when I arrived at the TASO Day Centre. They inquired how I had spent the night. I responded with a complaint of the constant diarrhea that bothered and depressed me. I was informed that it was a common problem with HIV patients, but I was reassured that it would clear with proper and constant treatment. This encouraged me and I was relieved to know that I was not alone in this problem.

After a while, I realized that everyone was busily engaged in some activity or another. In one corner, a group was playing games. Others were at the sewing machines, some making bed sheets, others school bags or shorts, and yet others were doing other handicrafts. I was invited to join in some activity and I decided on playing cards for a start. I took in all my surroundings and wondered if these people were actually in the same boat as me. The way they laughed, jested and cracked jokes made me wonder if they took their condition seriously.

At about 11 o'clock tea was served with some delicious pancakes, which I enjoyed very much. Not long after this, lunch was served. I had not realized the time had rushed by so fast. Lunch was a combination of rice and *matoke*, beef stew garnished with green vegetables, all well prepared, and pineapple as dessert. Just looking at the food encouraged my appetite. I marvelled at this generosity and the effort made to go to such limits. While we ate, some people cracked jokes about the virus. One lady in particular joked that she was going to compromise with her virus by feeding it so well that it would keep satisfied and forget to feed on her. In this way, her life would be prolonged and probably she would die a natural death. However she was determined never to let it out of her body to infect others. None of us could avoid laughing at such humour.

After lunch, I decided to have a go at the sewing machines. I was fortunate that I had taken tailoring during my teacher training course, so this was not new to me. I was surprised that I could still manage considering the one-and-a-half years that I had spent confined in bed. I had come to believe that I was too weak to do anything. But after being shown how to make a bag, I was amused when I managed to complete one by the end of the day.

I was saddened when it was announced that it was time to pack up and go home. I had wanted the day to go on endlessly. To my joy, the supervisor encouraged me to come whenever I can manage. With my heart full of joy, I left and resolved to make an effort to come regularly. My hopes were raised, and I realized that I had an enormous reserve of energies. With this hope and new outlook on life, I felt I could once again face the world with its challenges courageously. With the company of new found friends who accepted me unconditionally, I was determined I would shake off my fears. Depression and worry would remain at home in bed.

FRAN PEAVEY

USA

This is an excerpt from Fran Peavey's book A Shallow Pool of Time, *which is a record of her personal, political and spiritual insights on AIDS.*

Fran is a writer and a social activist with an involvement in global issues that pre-dates her HIV diagnosis. Fran began A Shallow Pool of Time *as a journal, to record the San Francisco gay and lesbian community as it faced the devastation of AIDS. However in the midst of keeping this record, she discovered that she herself was amongst those infected.*

Her piece is different from many others in this book because Fran clearly relates AIDS to environmental deterioration. She sees people living with AIDS as "the canaries in the mine," whistling a song so that we will know that "we must change our addiction to consumption, pollution and mindlessness."

I love to walk among great, old trees. Last summer a friend took me to a maple forest in Vermont. As we walked my friend told me that a healthy maple tree has a full leaf pattern in its outer perimeter, so its outline creates a solid, rather smooth line. You don't see spaces between the branches. From the jagged line of foliage on nearly all of the trees, it was easy to see that this forest was gravely ill. Like other forests in Canada and the Northeastern United States it has been poisoned by acid rain.

I hear that three-quarters of the people in my spiritual community in San Francisco have the AIDS virus in their blood. On Sundays when I stand to sing, I look around and sense that I am standing in a dying forest. I miss trees from month to month. Friends are falling all around me.

We live in a world that is too polluted. There is not enough of an ozone layer left to protect us. Too much radioactivity has been released. New viruses mutate or are man-made; new conditions threaten our species.

It seems that we do not yet know how to mourn and let go when a whole way of life begins to die. Even when we can see that death, can know it from inside, it is difficult to believe that a new way of life must and will emerge. In these last years of the twentieth century, our old way of life has already begun its terminal decline, and yet we do not see a new birth arising.

We do not know how to mourn this death. So automatically, and in something of a frenzy, we cling to that which is mostly dead. It is our clinging that most surely will kill us, or at least speed the downward spiral.

Maybe we people who carry the AIDS virus are the canaries in the mine. Maybe we can whistle such a true and sweet song that our species will see that we must get out of the mine; we must change our addiction to consumption, pollution and mindlessness.

I, and thousands like me with viruses in our bodies, are waiting. This is not a passive waiting: we are not resigned to death. In many ways, we are busy doing whatever we can to increase our chances of "beating this thing," as Dennis put it. But there is a lot of waiting, too.

When I visited South Africa in 1986, I saw an entire society that was, in a sense, waiting. The black South Africans I spoke with showed a curious mixture of hope and hopelessness. They wait for possibility of change in the social contract between peoples. The white South Africans wait for that, too − sensing, perhaps dreading, the deep suffering and change that is in store for them when the inevitable spark comes. But they find hope within hopelessness as they look north at Zimbabwe where whites and blacks have passed through a revolution and now live in a new social arrangement where both racial groups participate in decisions in a way that is new for them.

The South Africans' way of waiting − of carrying on with faith and hope in the face of individually hopeless situations − was a perspective I personally had only dimly understood. It became clearer to me this summer as I wrestled with the waiting that lay before me, as I wondered what this AIDS virus was doing in my body. Contemplating my own future and our collective future − both very much in doubt − I asked myself, "How can I learn to wait, to sit with the devastating information which I now know?"

When I give talks or do comedy shows, people often approach me afterward to ask me about the future. They take me to a corner of the room and quietly say, "I hear that the environment is so destroyed that it cannot be reversed, that the end has already begun. Is that true?" They think somehow a comedian will know! Turning to comedians with questions like that is like putting clowns at the health centres to tell people whether they are HIV positive. (Maybe that's not a bad idea!) What can I tell these people? I have read about studies by the Worldwatch Institute and by the United Nations which indicate that some parts of our ecosystems and some species have been irreversibly destroyed. But who can know the extent of the damage? Our physical world is so complex and interconnected that the ramifications of any deterioration are significant and, I suspect, more extensive than most of us can comprehend.

And so we wait. Our waiting is directed toward a questionable future, one that seems to be closing in on the present and making it untenable. We are waiting for something we really don't want. We do everything we can to postpone the expected future. A friend of mine told me that before he knew he was HIV positive he jogged furiously every day, hoping that he could "outrun" the virus. As a species, we try to clean up toxic waste dumps and stop the clear cutting of the forests. We make every effort to preserve our health and our planet, but we also must wait, knowing the virus is already in the system, not yet knowing whether it is terminal or not. All actions may increase the odds that the ecosystem will not collapse completely before key changes can be brought into place.

Still, this waiting can feel like a passive activity. It produces in us feelings of powerlessness and vulnerability — infantile feelings — and we hate that. We rage against our powerlessness, our vulnerability, our having to wait. It is this rage that fuels the discussion of violent strategies in the AIDS community. In both instances, the rage is born of despair and a weariness of waiting while suffering continues.

In our times, there is a prevalent sense of "resignation," as Robert Lifton calls it. I occasionally taste the pungent flavour of that resignation myself. I have been looking at this resignation, within me, exploring it, trying to find out how to work with that resignation in order to allow my beak to harden so I can peck my way out of my egg and grow up and fly. It is a very tough task. In the early days of working against nuclear war and environmental destruction, I decided to ask myself every day the strategic question, "What can I do to help the world survive?" Since then I have made it my practice to get up usually between four and five in the morning sitting for an hour with that question, as well as practising loving people I am separated from.

I thought in 1979 that I might have to ask this question for many years without receiving any ideas from that life force inside and outside me. But I was willing to give the life force an opportunity to create answers and to develop my will by first walking answerless into the void of my morning sitting. I was prepared to do that for ten years without an answer. I said to myself that if at the end of that time no answer had come, I would re-evaluate. This is the tenth year of that practice. Fortunately some answers have arrived including comedy and other projects that I work on today. To be willing to ask strategic questions to which there are no known answers, and to wait — those are among the most difficult and heroic tasks we can do now. To continue to ask and consult that universal life force to direct us is, I believe, one of the most valuable beak-hardening and spiritually-maturing tasks we can do in our time.

We also must be willing to do whatever the life-force-from-within suggests. Often only a small thing comes clear in the morning meditation. I think it's important to carry out those small ideas in order to develop my "doing" muscles-to prove to myself and to the earth that I am standing ready. I am ready to make peace with my family members and friends; to do those intimate peacemaking tasks that are an ongoing part of life. At the same time, when big jobs come, I work through my shyness and small concept of myself enough to be able to say, "I'm ready."

When the opportunity came to help clean the Ganges, it was a real stretch for me and my small-town-Idaho sense of myself, but I had to say, "I'm ready." I wait, standing ready, asking every day for direction for the life force planted inside of me – and inside all beings – that can make a great difference in this crucial time.

Each of us can only do a very little to help the whole situation, but each small piece plays an important part in creating the whole shift.

It is important how we carry this waiting. Start paying attention to how you wait, the cost on your soul and the cost of this waiting on life around you. Find a way to smile on that waiting. For me, this is where my comedy comes from. I very much appreciate Thich Nhat Hanh's suggestion that we learn to smile on our own and others' suffering – not smiling derisively, but smiling as a way of joining ourselves to the suffering.

T.S. Eliot writes in his poem "East Coker" about waiting:

I said to my soul, be still, and wait without
    hope
For hope would be hope for the wrong thing;
    wait without love
For love would be love of the wrong thing;
    there is yet faith
But the faith and the love and the hope are all
    in the waiting.
Wait without thought, for you are not ready for
    thought:
So the darkness shall be the light, and the stillness the
    dancing.

It is so important to keep laughing in the midst of our waiting, in the midst of our fears and morbidity. Whatever we are dying of individually and collectively, whatever is happening to our forests, it is a key spiritual posture to smile upon our human condition. This, of course, does not preclude crying for the grief in the death, trembling with fear or raging in anger.

How can we allow the life force to inform and inspire us? We learn to wait and take very careful care of that bomb we carry inside of us. We can look at each other in our meetings and on the street. We can recognize each other. We are surrounded by people who are working to develop the muscle to do what has to be done – moving individually and collectively to meet the need. The old is dead, the new is not yet ready to be born. We are in the in-between time and so we wait.

We ask ourselves what time it is in our individual lives and in the life of our species. And we realize that we don't know. We tell ourselves stories, we lose ourselves in the whirl of everyday activities, we pretend that we are indifferent about the waiting and the toll it takes on us, we rehearse death's arrival, we affirm our faith in a transcendent power, we pray to spirits to intercede for us in the molding of the future. We invent magic and rituals to help us explore the meaning of waiting. But still we must wait.

Waiting becomes an allegory, a private purgatory in which our moral and psychic fibre is tested. We learn from waiting. We become disciplined, tough, hardened, stoic. And yet, in this waiting together we also find a kind of intimacy and loving that is rare in ordinary life. We experience interconnectedness. We are surprised by feelings of intense joy as we stand in a momentary shard of light.

Someday, perhaps, we will all be able to see what a non-political event this epidemic is; that it is not a matter of which populations are suffering and how far they are from our own; that no one is really unaffected. What a sweet illumination that will be! Come with me to a time distant in the future when our species can look back and see these present times, the AIDS virus, the people infected and afraid, the people non-infected and afraid, where we can see it all as past. How will our times look from a perspective in which we, fragile and vulnerable as well as strong and tough-beings now walking the streets in our tennis shoes, will be but dust for historians? Our plague will surely look much like plagues of other times — the black plague, the bubonic plague, polio and others. For AIDS too will be conquered, and new problems will arise until the earth is restored to health and the people learn to live together within reasonable limits of resources.

Someday we may know with confidence that our species is making the changes necessary for humans to live, and we may return in time to the normal mysteries of existence, love and a personal death in the natural order of things.

CAROLE LAFAVOUR

USA

Carole is a native woman from Minnesota. In her writing, she shows how AIDS has brought her closer to her community and her traditional spirituality. For her, AIDS is not a disruption of her life; instead it is part of her life's journey.

"Walking the Red Road" is about Indian spirituality. We chose it to end this book, because Carole has integrated AIDS into a vital and encompassing spiritual context.

It's very hard to describe the Indian way of spirituality and explain how it is we face the spirit world and understand its powers and ways.

Then, of course, explaining is only the half of it. How you hear it is the other. Can the hearer respect the sacred tobacco and eagle; are Cloudbeings understood; can protection be sought from the rainbow? I feel very honoured to be the "explainer" in this instance. You, the "healers" complete the circle.

My spirituality has been especially important to me as I've adjusted to having AIDS and incorporated it into my journey. Here's something about that.

Indian people view all experiences as spiritual. The sacred is inseparable from the "ordinary." So, for example, to kill an animal hunting, you must first offer tobacco as a sign of respect, asking the animal's permission, explaining why you want to do this, and that you take responsibility for it. Or, if you want to pick the wild asparagus you find in the woods, you again prayerfully ask permission and then pick only a part of the bunch, leaving enough of the "grandmothers and grandfathers" so they can multiply again.

Listen to an Igluck Eskimo: "The greatest part of life lies in the fact that human food consists entirely of souls. All the creatures that we have to kill and eat, all those that we have to strike down and destroy to make clothes for ourselves, have souls, souls that do not perish with the body."

This translates in my life today to respect for animal rights, prayers for food, avoiding wastefulness, grateful prayers for the herbal medicines I've taken. And spending time with all of those souls... alive!

Walking in the woods is relaxing to me, because of all the

loving spirits there. It's energizing because I know there are many healing spirits there.

Being a healer, a traditional healer, is a special gift from the Creator. Many tribes believe the bear was the first medicine person and it taught the two-leggeds. It is described by using BEAR as an acronym:

B balance — Sickness is spiritual as well as physical imbalance.
E everything — Circles expand and interact with each other. We are all cells of Mother Earth.
A acceptance — Respect for all living things and the diversity in life.
R ritual — Used to call power to focus on something. A place for emotional release in a safe environment.

A person is called to be a healer, a medicine person, sometimes preparing for it their whole life. Black Elk, the great medicine person of the Lakota, said: "Of course it was not I who cured. It was the power from the outer world. The visions and ceremonies had only made me like a hole through which the power could come to the two-leggeds. If I thought that I was doing it myself, the hole would close up and no power would come through."

I have been given many gifts of healing from medicine people, spiritual leaders, herbs, cardinals since I was diagnosed in late 1986 with ARC. Healing ceremonies, sweat lodges, medicines, as well as my daily prayers and meditations have pulled me through several crises in the past two years. And the love of family and friends here and around the country also has been very important in my healing because Indian People believe in the absolute sacredness of community.

On the journey of life, we are continually prepared for death as well as life. Death is greatly respected because it is inevitable. It is a time of transition. Chief Seattle said, "There is no death. Only a change of worlds."

The "Red Road" is a name used for the Indian way of spirituality. But really it's a way of life rather than just a way of spirituality. It directs my health, how I parent my daughter, how I view what I eat, the clothes I wear and my relationships.

The "Red Road" extends into death. After death, our soul continues its journey and is met and helped by the souls of relatives that have gone before. There is much joy and celebration.

It's trying to live life in balance. Without understanding the rhythms and cycles of all life, of Mother Earth and being respectful of them, human life (life of the two-leggeds) becomes disconnected. We live a life of dis-ease. As someone suggested, we (the world) is suffering from an immune deficiency.

It is futile and meaningless to make technological progress, take scientific giant steps, amass volumes of "things" ... and in the process lose our souls. Walking the Red Road did nothing less than transform my entire life; difficult sometimes, but the gifts are limitless.

To close my part of the circle, I'd like to share a morning prayer:

Great Spirit, I turn to the East for the gift of enlightenment, which opens my mind, removing the poisons that creep in and
prevent me from seeing the spirit in others, replacing the poison with clarity and honesty.

I turn to the South, the direction of renewal, innocence and rebirth that teaches we all can start life anew.

I turn to the West to the spirit of introspection, so I might reflect and act from that which springs from the center of my soul.

And to the North, whose spirit of wisdom opens us to faith and
trust in all living things; who nurtures the gift of wisdom. Megwetch (thank you) to the elders who teach us that all negative feelings – hatred, envy, prejudice, greed – are products of fear and that walking the Red Road helps cast those feelings out.

Megwetch to all living things that teach us the ways of humility
and perseverance. Megwetch to all living things that teach us about playfulness and the joy of being silly. Megwetch for each new day with its challenges and lessons, its gifts of knowledge and love. Great Spirit comfort all of us affected by AIDS.

OTHER BOOKS FROM SECOND STORY PRESS